Biodiversity Unveiled

Exploring India's Ecology, Evolution, and Conservation,

Dr. Anthonysamy David

Table of Contents

Acknowledgement

I would like to express my deepest gratitude to the many individuals and institutions who have supported me throughout the journey of writing this book.

First and foremost, I am profoundly thankful to **Xavier Institute of Natural Resources Management** at the Social Centre, Ahmednagar, Maharashtra, India. Your unwavering support and the resources provided were instrumental in the completion of this work. The vibrant intellectual environment at the institute has been a constant source of inspiration.

I am also deeply indebted to **Savitribai Phule Pune University** , under whose academic umbrella I have had the privilege to work. The University's commitment to excellence in education and research has greatly influenced the direction and depth of this book. The guidance and encouragement from my colleagues and mentors at the University have been invaluable.

I am very much indebted to my archbishop of Patna, Sebastian Kallupura, Vicar General Fr. James George, Treasurer Fr. Amalraj, and all my priest friends at Patna who always inspire me to write such a book. I also thank the provincial of Pune Jesuit Province and Fr. Stan Fernades, who always encourages and inspires me.

I extend my heartfelt thanks to my family and friends, whose patience, understanding, and encouragement have sustained me through the many hours of research and writing. Your belief in the importance of this work has been my driving force.

Special thanks to all the researchers, conservationists, and fieldworkers who have dedicated their lives to the study and preservation of India's rich biodiversity. Your tireless efforts have provided the foundation for much of the knowledge shared in these pages.

Dr. Anthonysamy David

Finally, I wish to acknowledge the countless species and ecosystems that make up the magnificent tapestry of life in India. This book is a tribute to the incredible diversity and resilience of life on our planet, and I hope it serves as a catalyst for its protection and conservation.

Thank you all for being part of this journey.

Dr. Anthony Samy David
Xavier Institute of Natural Resources Management
Ahmednagar, Maharashtra, India
Savitribai Phule Pune University

Copyright licence

Dr. Anthonysamy David

Foreword

B iodiversity Unveiled: Exploring
India's Ecology, Evolution, and
Conservation"

In a world where the pace of change is accelerating faster than ever, the delicate balance of life on Earth faces unprecedented challenges. Nowhere is this more evident than in India, a nation celebrated for its astonishingly diverse landscapes and the rich tapestry of life they support. **India's rich biodiversity** is both a blessing and a responsibility —a legacy that must be cherished, understood, and protected.

"Biodiversity Unveiled" comes at a critical moment, offering readers a comprehensive exploration of the forces that have shaped **India's ecosystems** and the urgent need for their preservation. As someone deeply committed to the study and conservation of biodiversity, I am honoured to write this foreword for a book that is not only timely but also essential.

In these pages, you will find a journey that spans millions of years and countless species, from the **Sundarbans Bengal tiger** to the towering trees of the Western Ghats. The book delves into the intricacies of **ecology and evolutionary biology**, providing a solid foundation for understanding how life has evolved and adapted in this diverse region. But it goes beyond the theoretical, bringing to life the practical side of **biodiversity conservation** with a focus on **applied biodiversity**.

India is home to some of the world's most unique and fragile ecosystems. The **biogeography of India** is a story of isolation, migration, and adaptation, with each region harbouring species found nowhere else on Earth. Understanding this complexity is key to protecting these ecosystems from the threats they face today—deforestation, climate change, and human encroachment. This book provides the tools and insights necessary to tackle these challenges head-on.

But "Biodiversity Unveiled" is not just for scientists and conservationists. It is for anyone who cares about the future of our planet and the life it sustains. The stories of **nature conservation** and **environmental protection** in India are stories of hope, resilience, and determination. They remind us that while the challenges are great, the efforts to overcome them are equally powerful.

The authors of this book have succeeded in weaving together a narrative that is both informative and inspiring. They have managed to capture the essence of **India's natural heritage** while also providing a clear call to action. As you read through the chapters, you will not only gain knowledge but also a deep appreciation for the interconnectedness of life and the urgent need to protect it.

In a time when the natural world is under siege, "Biodiversity Unveiled" stands as a beacon of knowledge and hope. It reminds us that the battle to conserve our planet's biodiversity is not just a scientific endeavour but a moral imperative. I urge you to take this journey, to immerse yourself in the wonders of **India's rich biodiversity** , and to join the global effort to ensure that these treasures are preserved for generations to come.

This book is a testament to the power of knowledge and the importance of action. May it inspire you, as it has inspired me, to continue the work of conserving the incredible diversity of life that makes our world so vibrant and so precious.

Prologue

Biodiversity Unveiled: Exploring India's Ecology, Evolution, and Conservation"

In the vast and varied landscapes of India, life thrives in forms and numbers that boggle the mind. From the towering Himalayas to the dense mangroves of the Sundarbans, India is a living testament to nature's incredible ability to adapt, evolve, and flourish. This country is not just a patchwork of ecosystems but a tapestry woven with threads of history, culture, and life that span millions of years.

Yet, this extraordinary richness— **India's rich biodiversity** —is under threat. Rapid development, climate change, and human encroachment are placing unprecedented pressures on ecosystems that have existed for millennia. The **Sundarbans Bengal tiger** now finds itself on the brink, the once-abundant rivers are struggling to sustain life, and ancient forests are giving way to concrete jungles. The urgency to understand, protect, and preserve **India's natural heritage** has never been greater.

This book, "Biodiversity Unveiled," is born out of that urgency. It is an invitation to explore the intricate world of **ecology and evolutionary biology** , to understand the forces that have shaped life in this region, and to grasp the importance of **biodiversity conservation** in our rapidly changing world. We delve into the **biogeography of India** , tracing the pathways through which species have spread and adapted, and the unique ecological niches they have carved out.

In these pages, we will also examine **applied biodiversity** —the practical strategies and innovations that scientists, conservationists, and local communities are employing to protect **India's**

ecosystems . From grassroots movements to large-scale governmental efforts, the battle to conserve our environment is as diverse and complex as the ecosystems themselves.

But this book is more than just a scientific exploration; it is a call to action. As we journey through the mangroves, forests, and plains of India, we will encounter stories of resilience, hope, and dedication. Stories of individuals and communities who are fighting to ensure that the wonders of nature can be passed on to future generations. This is not just a book for academics or conservationists —it is for anyone who believes in the power of nature, the beauty of life, and the necessity of **environmental protection** .

As you turn these pages, I invite you to see the world through the eyes of a Bengal tiger stalking through the Sundarbans, to feel the pulse of life in the forests of the Western Ghats, and to understand the delicate balance that sustains this diversity of life. **India's rich biodiversity** is a treasure, and it is up to us to protect it.

Dr. Anthonysamy David

Let this book be your guide as we explore, learn, and ultimately act to preserve the magnificent tapestry that is **India's natural heritage** . The journey begins here.

Chapter 1

Ecology and Evolutionary Biology

Understanding ecology and evolutionary biology is essential for comprehending the complex dynamics of life on Earth. Ecology focuses on how organisms interact with each other and their environment, exploring relationships within ecosystems and how they sustain themselves. In contrast, evolutionary biology examines the origins and transformations of species over time, providing insights into the mechanisms driving biodiversity. Together, these fields offer a comprehensive view of natural systems, highlighting the interconnectedness of all living entities and emphasising the significance of preserving diverse biological systems.

Dr. Anthonysamy David

This chapter delves into the intricate relationships that define ecosystems, examining interactions such as predation, competition, mutualism, and parasitism among various organisms. It also considers the influence of abiotic factors like climate and soil on the distribution and behaviour of species. Furthermore, the chapter explores the principles of evolutionary biology, including natural selection and adaptation, to elucidate the processes that shape biodiversity. By integrating ecological and evolutionary perspectives, the chapter underscores the importance of eco-evolutionary dynamics in conservation efforts, offering valuable insights for researchers, environmentalists, biologists, and others interested in understanding and protecting our planet's biological diversity.

Ecology and Evolutionary Biology

Ecology and evolutionary biology are both crucial fields in understanding the intricate dynamics of life on Earth. Ecology investigates the interactions between organisms and their surrounding environment, helping us comprehend how ecosystems function and sustain themselves. Evolutionary biology, on the other hand, delves into the origins and transformations of species over time, providing insights into the mechanisms that drive biodiversity. Together, these disciplines offer a holistic view of natural systems, emphasising the interconnectedness of all living things.

Ecology is fundamentally about relationships. It seeks to understand how different organisms interact with one another and with their physical surroundings. These interactions can be classified into various types, including predation, competition, mutualism, and parasitism. For example, the relationship between a predator and its prey highlights the dynamic balance within ecosystems. When predators hunt and consume prey, they help regulate prey populations, preventing overgrazing or depletion of resources. Similarly, plants and pollinators engage in mutualistic relationships where both parties benefit —plants receive assistance in reproduction through pollination, while pollinators gain nourishment from nectar.

Moreover, ecology considers abiotic factors like climate, soil, and water, which significantly influence the distribution and behaviour of organisms. For instance, temperature and precipitation patterns determine the types of vegetation that can thrive in an area, which in turn affects the animal species that can inhabit those regions. Understanding these ecological interactions allows scientists to predict how changes in environmental conditions might impact biodiversity and ecosystem stability.

Evolutionary biology complements this by focusing on the history and development of life forms. It traces the ancestry of species, examining how genetic variations arise and propagate across generations. The theory of evolution posits that species evolve through processes such as mutation, gene flow, genetic drift, and, most notably, natural selection. Natural selection acts on the heritable traits of individuals, favouring those better adapted to their environments. Over time, these advantageous traits become more prevalent in the population, leading to evolutionary changes.

A pivotal concept in evolutionary biology is adaptation. Adaptations are traits that enhance an organism's ability to survive and reproduce in specific environments. For example, the thick fur of polar bears is an adaptation to the frigid Arctic climate, providing insulation against the cold. In a contrasting environment, cacti have evolved thickened stems to store water, enabling them to endure arid desert conditions. These adaptations result from selective pressures exerted by the environment, illustrating the principle of survival of the fittest.

Understanding natural selection and adaptation sheds light on the vast diversity of life on Earth. The constant interaction of evolutionary forces shapes biodiversity, which is the variety of life in all its forms, from genes to species to ecosystems. Diverse ecosystems are more resilient to disturbances because they contain a wide array of species with different roles and functions. For example, a forest with numerous plant species can better withstand pest outbreaks, as some plants may possess resistance traits that others lack. This diversity also facilitates ecological processes like nutrient cycling and energy flow, ensuring the sustainability of the ecosystem.

The interaction between ecological and evolutionary processes is a vital area of study. Eco-evolutionary dynamics refers to how ecological interactions (like competition and predation) and evolutionary changes (such as adaptations) influence each other. For instance, the introduction of a new predator can exert selective pressure on prey species, driving the evolution of defensive traits. Conversely, evolutionary changes in prey can alter predator-prey dynamics, affecting population sizes and community structure.

In applied biology, understanding eco-evolutionary dynamics has practical implications. For instance, conservation efforts often aim to mitigate mismatches between current phenotypes and environmental conditions, enhancing population fitness and size (Hendry et al., 2011). Moreover, strategies to combat pests or pathogens may involve increasing evolutionary mismatches, thereby reducing their fitness and prevalence.

One real-world application of evolutionary principles is in agriculture, where breeding programmes harness genetic variation to develop crops with desirable traits such as disease resistance and high yield. By selecting and propagating these beneficial traits, agricultural productivity can be optimised, demonstrating the utility of evolutionary concepts in human endeavours (Hendry et al., 2011).

Additionally, evolutionary biology provides critical insights into medical science. Understanding the evolution of antibiotic resistance helps in developing strategies to reduce the spread of resistant strains. For instance, rotating different classes of antibiotics can minimise the selective pressure on bacterial populations, slowing resistance evolution. Similarly, evolutionary principles guide the design of vaccines and treatments that anticipate the adaptive responses of pathogens.

Dr. Anthonysamy David

Flora and Fauna: Diversity in Species

The diversity within plant and animal species is immense, reflecting the rich tapestry of life on Earth. To appreciate this, we must first understand the basic classification of species into flora and fauna. Flora refers to plants, encompassing everything from towering trees to microscopic algae. Fauna, on the other hand, denotes animals, ranging from mammals and birds to insects and marine life.

Diverse plant species play crucial roles in ecosystems. For instance, the Amazon Rainforest is home to over 40,000 different plant species (National Geographic Society, 2012). These plants provide oxygen, food, and habitat for countless other organisms. Trees like the Brazil nut tree support entire ecosystems by offering fruits eaten by various animals, which in turn disperse the seeds, ensuring forest regeneration. In grasslands, grasses such as buffalo grass help maintain soil health and prevent erosion, supporting herbivores that graze on them. Wetland plants like cattails filter water, reducing pollution and providing habitat for birds and amphibians.

Animal species exhibit a vast range of ecological niches, each with unique adaptations. For example, the African elephant plays a vital role in savannas and forests by creating clearings that promote plant growth, which benefits other species. Predators like the Bengal tiger regulate prey populations, maintaining ecological balance. In marine environments, coral reefs built by tiny polyps provide shelter for diverse fish species, contributing to the high biodiversity in places like the Bird's Head Seascape in Indonesia (National Geographic Society, 2012).

Genetic diversity within species is equally critical for survival and adaptability. Genes, the units of biological information passed down through generations, vary among individuals within a species. This genetic variation is why individual dogs can be poodles or pit bulls, and humans can have different eye colours (National Geographic Society, 2012). Greater genetic diversity equips species to withstand diseases and adapt to environmental changes. For example, during the American chestnut blight in the early 1900s, the forest ecosystem survived because other tree species also grew there (National Geographic Society, 2012). Similarly, crop diversity ensures food security, as different varieties can resist pests and climate variations.

Human Impact on Biodiversity

Human activities have undeniably shaped the landscape of our planet, often to the detriment of biodiversity. Examining how these actions affect biodiversity requires a multi-faceted approach, focusing on economic and industrial factors, technological advancements, cultural and governance aspects, and the broader impacts of globalisation.

Firstly, economic and industrial activities are primary drivers of habitat loss and species decline. The transformation of natural habitats into agricultural lands has been significant, driven by the need to produce food for a growing population. According to research, large-scale food production accounts for approximately 30% of global biodiversity decline (The Royal Society, 2024). This transformation not only involves deforestation but also the fragmentation of remaining habitats, which isolates species populations and reduces their genetic diversity. Industrial activities, such as mining and infrastructure development, further exacerbate this situation by converting vast areas of natural ecosystems into industrial zones. For instance, the overexploitation of natural resources for timber and minerals depletes habitats and directly contributes to species loss. Pollution from industrial processes, including the widespread use of pesticides and fertilisers, contaminates soil and water, rendering these environments hostile to many forms of life.

Guideline: To mitigate these effects, it is essential for policymakers to implement regulations that balance economic growth with ecological preservation. Encouraging sustainable farming practices, reducing industrial pollution, and protecting critical habitats through legislation are vital measures.

Technological advancements present both opportunities and threats to biodiversity. On one hand, technologies in monitoring and conservation efforts have proven invaluable. Remote sensing and satellite imagery enable researchers to track changes in land use and identify critical areas for conservation. Genetic engineering has allowed the development of crops that require fewer resources, potentially reducing the strain on natural habitats. However, technology also facilitates activities that harm biodiversity. Advances in fishing equipment, for example, have led to overfishing, depleting marine populations at an unprecedented rate. Similarly, modern transportation systems have accelerated the spread of invasive species, which can outcompete native species and disrupt ecosystems. Climate change, driven by technological reliance on fossil fuels, compounds these issues by altering habitats and forcing species to migrate or adapt rapidly.

Guidelines: It is crucial to leverage technological advancements responsibly. Investing in green technologies, promoting research on alternative energy sources, and enforcing stringent controls on invasive species are necessary steps.

Cultural and governance frameworks play a significant role in biodiversity conservation. Cultural values influence how societies interact with their natural environments. In some cultures, traditional practices and beliefs foster a symbiotic relationship with nature, guiding sustainable resource use. Governance structures determine the effectiveness of conservation policies and the enforcement of environmental laws. Countries with robust legal frameworks and engaged civil society organisations tend to manage their natural resources more sustainably. Conversely, weak governance can lead to inadequate protection of biodiversity and exploitation of natural resources. Corruption and lack of transparency further undermine conservation efforts, allowing illegal activities like poaching and unregulated logging to persist.

Guidelines: Strengthening governance systems and integrating cultural values into conservation strategies are essential. Ensuring community involvement in decision-making processes, providing education on sustainable practices, and enhancing transparency in resource management can significantly boost conservation outcomes.

Lastly, globalisation has far-reaching consequences for ecosystems and species distribution. The interconnectedness of global markets drives economic activities that often lead to environmental degradation. The demand for products such as palm oil, soy, and beef incentivizes the expansion of agriculture into previously undisturbed areas. Global trade not only accelerates habitat conversion but also increases greenhouse gas emissions, contributing to climate change and further impacting biodiversity. Additionally, globalisation facilitates the rapid movement of species across borders, leading to biological invasions. These non-native species can become invasive, displacing indigenous flora and fauna and causing irreversible damage to local ecosystems.

Globalisation also influences species distribution by altering migration patterns. Climate change, a byproduct of global industrial activity, forces many species to shift their ranges in search of suitable habitats. Some species may benefit from new environments, while others face extinction due to their inability to adapt quickly enough. The homogenization of ecosystems, driven by the global spread of similar land-use practices, reduces the unique characteristics of different habitats, further diminishing biodiversity.

Conservation of Biodiversity

Conserving biodiversity is essential for maintaining ecological balance and sustaining the well-being of our planet. Various strategies and approaches have been developed to address this critical issue. Among these, in-situ and ex-situ conservation methods play a significant role.

Dr. Anthonysamy David

In-situ conservation involves protecting species within their natural habitats. This method focuses on establishing protected areas like national parks, wildlife reserves, and marine protected zones where ecosystems can function without human interference. One of the strengths of in-situ conservation is that it maintains the entire ecosystem intact, preserving the complex interactions between different species. However, the success of this approach depends heavily on adequate land management and protection from external threats such as poaching or habitat destruction.

Ex-situ conservation, on the other hand, takes place outside the natural habitats of species. This includes practices like captive breeding programmes, botanical gardens, and seed banks. Ex-situ conservation is often used when species are critically endangered and immediate intervention is required to prevent extinction. While ex-situ methods provide a controlled environment for breeding and research, they may not always replicate the intricate conditions of an organism's natural habitat, which can present challenges for reintroduction into the wild.

Preserving endangered species and their habitats is paramount for biodiversity conservation. The loss of even a single species can have cascading effects on an entire ecosystem. For example, the disappearance of a keystone species, such as the sea otter, which preys on sea urchins, can lead to the overpopulation of urchins and the subsequent destruction of kelp forests. Preserving habitats ensures that species can continue to interact with their environment in ways that support ecological stability and resilience.

Global conservation efforts and international agreements are indispensable in addressing biodiversity loss on a broader scale. Agreements like the Convention on Biological Diversity (CBD) set international targets for the conservation and sustainable use of biodiversity. Additionally, organisations such as the International Union for Conservation of Nature (IUCN) work globally to monitor species' statuses and promote conservation actions. These initiatives encourage countries to collaborate and share resources, knowledge, and technologies to protect biodiversity more effectively.

Community participation and education are critical components of successful conservation efforts. Local communities often have profound knowledge about their environment and can offer valuable insights into sustainable resource management practices. Engaging communities in conservation projects not only helps to build local capacity but also fosters a sense of ownership and responsibility towards natural resources. Educational programmes raise awareness about the importance of biodiversity and inspire community members to participate actively in conservation activities.

An excellent example of community-based conservation is the establishment of community conservancies in Namibia. Here, local communities manage wildlife resources and benefit economically through ecotourism. This model has led to increased wildlife populations and improved livelihoods, demonstrating the potential of community involvement in conservation.

Education also plays a pivotal role in shaping public attitudes towards conservation. Informal educational settings, such as museums, zoos, and aquariums, can introduce people to the concept of biodiversity and its importance. School curricula integrating environmental science can instil values of conservation from a young age. When individuals understand the significance of biodiversity and the threats it faces, they are more likely to support and engage in conservation efforts.

Furthermore, integrating green policies and sustainable development practices at all levels of governance can significantly bolster conservation efforts. Governments can implement regulations to protect natural areas, control pollution, and promote the sustainable use of resources. Incentives for businesses engaging in environmentally friendly practices can encourage wider adoption of sustainable methods. By aligning economic development with environmental sustainability, governments can help secure the future of biodiversity.

Conservation approaches must also consider geographical factors. The location and design of conservation areas influence their effectiveness. For instance, creating a network of connected habitats allows species to migrate safely, adapt to changing conditions and find new sources of food and shelter. Such connectivity is crucial in regions experiencing rapid environmental changes due to climate change.

Climate Change and Greenhouse Gas Effects

The greenhouse gas effect is a critical phenomenon contributing to global warming. It involves gases like carbon dioxide, methane, and nitrous oxide trapping heat in the Earth's atmosphere, leading to an increase in global temperatures. These gases allow sunlight to enter the atmosphere freely, but they trap the heat that the Earth radiates back into space. This trapped heat leads to a warming effect, which significantly influences climatic patterns and subsequently impacts biodiversity.

Climate change induced by greenhouse gases has direct and indirect effects on species and ecosystems. Directly, rising temperatures can alter habitats, making them unsuitable for some species while making others more adaptable to heat. For instance, polar bears are losing their icy habitats due to melting ice caps, whereas some pest populations thrive with warmer conditions, threatening crops and native plant species. Indirect effects include changes in food availability and interspecies relationships. Warmer temperatures can cause a shift in the distribution of plant species, altering the food sources for herbivores and subsequently affecting the predators that feed on these herbivores.

Extreme weather events and shifting climate patterns pose significant risks to biodiversity. Hurricanes, droughts, and floods are becoming more frequent and intense, disrupting ecosystems and leading to a loss of habitat. Coral reefs, for example, are highly sensitive to temperature changes; prolonged exposure to high temperatures causes coral bleaching, where corals expel the algae living in their tissues, often leading to the death of coral reefs. Shifting climate patterns also result in unpredictable growing seasons, affecting agricultural productivity and natural vegetation cycles, which can have cascading effects on the entire ecosystem.

Mitigation and adaptation strategies are essential for reducing the impacts of climate change on biodiversity. Mitigation involves measures to reduce or prevent the emission of greenhouse gases, such as transitioning to renewable energy sources, enhancing energy efficiency, and implementing reforestation projects. By reducing emissions, we can slow down global warming and lessen its adverse effects on ecosystems. Adaptation strategies focus on adjusting practices, processes, and structures to minimise harm from climate change. This can include creating wildlife corridors to allow species to migrate safely, managing water resources more efficiently, and developing resilient agricultural practices that can withstand changing climate conditions.

One effective mitigation measure is the implementation of carbon sequestration practices. Carbon sequestration involves capturing atmospheric carbon dioxide and storing it in plants, soil, or underground reservoirs. Forests play a vital role in this process, as trees absorb carbon dioxide during photosynthesis. Protecting existing forests and planting new ones can significantly contribute to carbon sequestration efforts. Additionally, innovative technologies such as carbon capture and storage (CCS) at industrial sites help prevent large amounts of CO_2 from entering the atmosphere.

Adaptation also requires focusing on preserving genetic diversity within species. Genetic diversity allows species to adapt to environmental changes and resist diseases, enhancing their chances of survival in changing climates. Conservation programmes aimed at protecting endangered species and maintaining healthy population sizes are crucial. Breeding programmes for endangered species, coupled with habitat restoration, can help maintain biodiversity and ecological balance.

Another adaptation strategy is the development of sustainable agriculture practices. Traditional farming methods are often not resilient to climate change impacts. Sustainable practices include crop rotation, agroforestry, and organic farming, which improve soil health and reduce dependency on chemical inputs. These methods enhance the ability of agricultural systems to withstand extreme weather conditions and ensure food security while protecting biodiversity.

Marine ecosystems also require special attention due to their vulnerability to climate change. Ocean acidification, caused by increased CO_2 absorption, and rising sea temperatures threaten marine life, particularly shellfish and coral species. Establishing marine protected areas (MPAs) can help conserve ocean biodiversity by restricting human activities that damage marine habitats. MPAs provide refuges where marine life can recover and thrive, contributing to healthier and more resilient ocean ecosystems.

Implementing policies that support both mitigation and adaptation is essential for long-term success. Governments and international organisations must collaborate to set ambitious targets for reducing greenhouse gas emissions and invest in research and development of new technologies. Public awareness campaigns can also play a significant role in promoting environmentally friendly practices among individuals and communities.

Bringing It All Together

In this chapter, we have explored the complex dynamics within biological systems through the lenses of ecology and evolutionary biology. We examined how organisms interact with each other and their environments, highlighted the significance of adaptation and natural selection, and discussed the interconnected roles that biodiversity plays in maintaining ecosystem health. These fundamental concepts help us understand the intricate web of life on Earth and underscore the importance of preserving these relationships for future generations.

The impact of human activities on biodiversity has also been a critical point of discussion. Industrialisation, technological advancements, cultural practices, and globalisation all pose challenges to the conservation of diverse species and their habitats. By understanding these influences and employing targeted conservation strategies—such as in-situ and ex-situ conservation methods, community involvement, and international agreements—we can work towards mitigating these impacts. Addressing climate change through both mitigation and adaptation efforts is crucial to safeguarding the planet's biodiversity. The chapter emphasises the need for collective action and responsible management to ensure the sustainability of our natural world.

Reference List

Bera, B. (2022). *In-situ and ex-situ strategy for biodiversity conservation* . *FUNDAMENTALS OF BIODIVERSITY* , 115-169. Retrieved from https://www.researchgate.net/publication/371154727_In-situ_and_Ex-situ_Strategy_forBiodiversity_Conservation

Biodiversity and natural selection (video) . (n.d.). Khan Academy. https://www.khanacademy.org/science/ap-biology/natural-selection/natural-selection-ap/v/biodiversity-and-natural-selection-two

Center for Biological Diversity. (2019). *The Elements of Biodiversity* . Biologicaldiversity.org. https://www.biologicaldiversity.org/programs/biodiversity/elements_of_biodiversity/

Dr. Anthonysamy David

ESS Topic 3.4: Conservation of Biodiversity . (n.d.). AMAZING WORLD of SCIENCE with MR. GREEN. https://www.mrgscience.com/ess-topic-34-conservation-of-biodiversity.html

Hendry, A. P., Kinnison, M. T., Heino, M., Day, T., Smith, T. B., Fitt, G., Bergstrom, C. T., Oakeshott, J., Jørgensen, P. S., Zalucki, M. P., Gilchrist, G., Southerton, S., Sih, A., Strauss, S., Denison, R. F., & Carroll, S. P. (2011, February 17). *Evolutionary principles and their practical application* . Evolutionary Applications. https://doi.org/10.1111/j.1752-4571.2010.00165.x

Hostetter, T. (2012). *Human Impact on Biodiversity* . Goshen.edu. https://www.goshen.edu/bio/Biol410/bsspapers05/Trishahostette.htm

National Geographic Society. (2012, October 9). *Biodiversity* . National Geographic Society; National Geographic Society. https://www.nationalgeographic.org/encyclopedia/biodiversity/

The Royal Society. (2024). *What is the human impact on biodiversity? | Royal Society* . Royalsociety.org. https://royalsociety.org/news-resources/projects/biodiversity/human-impact-on-biodiversity/

Chapter 2

Perspectives and Approaches Towards Biodiversity

Understanding the various perspectives and approaches towards biodiversity is essential for effective conservation efforts. Biodiversity management occurs at multiple levels, each with unique strategies and stakeholder involvement. From international treaties to local community initiatives, these approaches are designed to protect the planet's biological diversity, which is fundamental to ecosystem stability and human well-being. Diverse methods are used to maintain biodiversity registers, providing a comprehensive database necessary for informed decision-making and policy formulation.

This chapter delves into several key aspects of biodiversity management. It explores how international frameworks set the stage for national and local strategies by offering guidelines and facilitating cooperation among countries. The role and responsibilities of different stakeholders, including government agencies, NGOs, the private sector, and indigenous communities, are examined in depth. Moreover, the chapter discusses various techniques for maintaining biodiversity registers, highlighting the importance of accurate data collection and management. By addressing these topics, the chapter provides a holistic view of the efforts required to sustain and enhance global biodiversity.

International Approaches to Biodiversity

International efforts in biodiversity conservation have been pivotal in setting frameworks and strategies that guide and aid countries globally in their conservation endeavours. One of the cornerstones of these international efforts is the establishment of treaties like the Convention on Biological Diversity (CBD), which sets global standards for conservation practices. Adopted during the Earth Summit in Rio de Janeiro in 1992, the CBD aims at promoting sustainable development and ensuring the fair and equitable sharing of benefits arising from genetic resources. This treaty plays a crucial role in encouraging nations to develop their own biodiversity strategies and action plans while aligning them with global goals.

Another significant entity in international biodiversity conservation is the United Nations Environment Programme (UNEP). UNEP coordinates numerous global initiatives, bringing together governments, NGOs, and other stakeholders to work towards common conservation goals. The Kunming-Montreal Global Biodiversity Framework (KMGBF), also known as The Biodiversity Plan, adopted under the umbrella of the CBD, exemplifies UNEP's role in spearheading large-scale environmental projects aimed at halting and reversing biodiversity loss by 2030. Through various programmes and partnerships, UNEP facilitates knowledge exchange, develops policy recommendations, and provides technical support to countries, ensuring cohesive efforts in biodiversity conservation.

Multinational research collaborations further enhance international efforts to understand and address biodiversity loss. Collaborative research projects allow scientists from different countries to share data, methodologies, and findings, leading to a more comprehensive understanding of complex ecological issues. For example, initiatives such as the Intergovernmental Science-Policy Platform on Biodiversity and Ecosystem Services (IPBES) rely on contributions from an extensive network of experts worldwide to provide assessments and advice on biodiversity-related matters. These collaborations often result in innovative solutions and strategies that individual countries might struggle to develop independently.

Dr. Anthonysamy David

Financial mechanisms are another vital component supporting global biodiversity efforts. The Global Environment Facility (GEF) is one of the most prominent financial mechanisms dedicated to funding biodiversity projects. Established in 1991, GEF provides grants and mobilises co-financing for projects that address critical environmental issues, including biodiversity conservation. By pooling resources from multiple donor countries, GEF ensures that funds are available to implement large-scale conservation projects, especially in developing countries where financial constraints often hinder environmental initiatives. Moreover, the GEF plays a significant role in facilitating the implementation of international agreements like the CBD by providing necessary financial support and technical assistance to participating countries.

International treaties such as the Convention on Biological Diversity (CBD) establish essential guidelines for conservation efforts globally. The CBD not only outlines key objectives for biodiversity conservation but also provides a platform for countries to share best practices and enhance cooperation. Through its Conferences of the Parties (COP) meetings, the CBD enables member states to review progress, set new targets, and address emerging challenges in biodiversity conservation. This dynamic approach ensures that the global community remains committed to achieving sustainable development goals related to biodiversity.

The United Nations Environment Programme (UNEP) significantly impacts by harmonising international activities geared towards biodiversity conservation. UNEP's strategic initiatives, such as the Sustainable Ocean Initiative (SOI) Global Dialogue, illustrate its efforts to foster collaboration among various stakeholders, including governments, non-governmental organisations, and local communities. By facilitating dialogues and partnerships, UNEP helps create synergies that amplify the impact of conservation actions taken at the national and regional levels.

In addition to organisational efforts, multinational research collaborations contribute substantially to addressing biodiversity issues. Projects like the

Global Biodiversity Information Facility (GBIF) highlight the importance of shared data repositories, enabling researchers worldwide to access and contribute to a collective pool of biodiversity information. Such collaborations not only enhance the quality and scope of biodiversity data but also promote transparency and inclusivity in scientific research. Consequently, these efforts lead to more informed decision-making processes and effective conservation strategies.

Financial mechanisms like the Global Environment Facility (GEF) play a crucial role in supporting biodiversity projects, particularly in financially constrained regions. GEF's funding strategy encompasses a diverse range of projects, from habitat restoration to sustainable agriculture, ensuring a holistic approach to biodiversity conservation. In recent years, GEF has also focused on innovative financing solutions, such as blended finance models, which combine public and private sector investments to maximise the impact of conservation projects. This approach not only leverages additional resources but also encourages greater involvement from various sectors in biodiversity conservation.

Furthermore, the integration of international biodiversity initiatives into national policies enhances the effectiveness of conservation efforts. Countries are encouraged to align their national biodiversity strategies with global frameworks like the CBD and KMGBF, ensuring consistency and coherence in their approach. This alignment helps streamline conservation actions across different levels of governance and promotes the efficient use of resources. Additionally, it fosters a sense of shared responsibility and accountability among nations, driving collective action towards common conservation goals.

Public awareness and education are also critical components of international biodiversity efforts. Campaigns and educational initiatives run by organizations like UNEP aim to increase awareness of the value of biodiversity and the urgent need for its conservation. These initiatives target various audiences, from policymakers to the general public, emphasising the interconnectedness of human well-being and biodiversity health. By fostering a deeper understanding of biodiversity issues, these efforts encourage more active participation in conservation activities and support for relevant policies.

Lastly, international efforts in biodiversity conservation are continually evolving to address emerging challenges and opportunities. Adaptive management practices, driven by ongoing research and technological advancements, enable the global community to respond effectively to changing ecological conditions. Initiatives such as the adoption of digital tools and satellite monitoring systems enhance the ability to track biodiversity changes and implement timely conservation measures. As these efforts advance, they pave the way for a more resilient and sustainable future for the planet's biodiversity.

National-level strategies for Biodiversity

National efforts to manage biodiversity conservation are multifaceted, involving strategic planning, legislative measures, cross-sectoral integration, and robust monitoring systems. This subpoint aims to explore how nations navigate these critical areas to maintain and enhance biodiversity within their territories.

One of the cornerstone initiatives in national biodiversity management is the development and implementation of National Biodiversity Strategies and Action Plans (NBSAPs). These plans serve as comprehensive frameworks that guide national efforts in conservation. NBSAPs are often aligned with international biodiversity targets and goals, such as those set by the Convention on Biological Diversity. They outline specific actions, targets, and timelines that countries adopt to preserve and protect their biological resources. For instance, many countries have committed to setting aside a percentage of their land and marine areas as protected zones, which are managed to conserve ecosystems and species. Adherence to these plans ensures that conservation activities are systematic, coherent, and effective across different regions and scales (Unit, n.d.).

Laws and regulations form another essential pillar in the management of biodiversity conservation at the national level. Governments enforce various legal mechanisms to protect endangered species and habitats. These laws may include restrictions on hunting, fishing, and trading of threatened species, as well as regulations on land use and development in ecologically sensitive areas. For example, the Endangered Species Act in the United States provides comprehensive protection for species identified as at risk of extinction. It includes measures for habitat preservation, recovery plans, and penalties for non-compliance. Such regulatory frameworks create an enforceable structure within which biodiversity can be safeguarded and managed effectively.

Integrating biodiversity considerations into other sectors like agriculture, forestry, and urban development is crucial for holistic conservation efforts. This cross-sectoral approach ensures that biodiversity is not seen in isolation but as an integral component of various economic activities. In agriculture, practices such as agroforestry and organic farming promote sustainable use of land resources while conserving biodiversity. Forestry management plans often incorporate conservation strategies like selective logging and maintaining buffer zones around critical habitats. Urban development projects increasingly consider green spaces, wildlife corridors, and sustainable infrastructure to minimise their impact on local ecosystems. By embedding biodiversity considerations into multiple sectors, countries can achieve more balanced and sustainable development.

Monitoring and reporting systems play a pivotal role in tracking biodiversity changes at the national level. These systems involve the collection, analysis, and dissemination of data on various aspects of biodiversity, such as species population trends, habitat conditions, and genetic diversity. National biodiversity monitoring programmes often utilise a range of tools and technologies, including geographic information systems (GIS), remote sensing, and citizen science initiatives. For example, the European Environment Agency's Biodiversity Data Centre collates information from diverse sources to provide comprehensive reports on the status and trends of biodiversity across Europe. Effective monitoring enables countries to assess the effectiveness of their conservation policies and make informed decisions based on up-to-date scientific evidence.

In designing NBSAPs, countries often engage in extensive stakeholder consultations to ensure that the plans are inclusive and address the needs of different groups. This process not only builds ownership and commitment among stakeholders but also leverages their knowledge and expertise. For instance, indigenous communities frequently play a vital role in biodiversity conservation due to their traditional ecological knowledge and sustainable practices. Incorporating their insights into NBSAPs can lead to more culturally appropriate and effective conservation strategies.

Government agencies tasked with enforcing biodiversity laws often work closely with other stakeholders, such as non-governmental organisations (NGOs), academic institutions, and local communities. This collaborative approach enhances the implementation and enforcement of conservation measures. NGOs, for example, may assist in monitoring illegal activities, conducting research, and raising awareness about biodiversity issues. Academic institutions can contribute through research and innovation, providing new insights and solutions for conservation challenges. Local communities, as custodians of their natural environment, are essential partners in implementing conservation actions on the ground.

The integration of biodiversity considerations into sectors like agriculture and urban development requires policy coherence and coordination among different government ministries and departments. Agriculture ministries, for example, need to work in tandem with environmental agencies to promote sustainable farming practices that support biodiversity. Similarly, urban planning authorities must collaborate with conservation bodies to design cities that are environmentally friendly and resilient. Policymakers face the challenge of balancing economic growth and development with the need to preserve biodiversity. This often involves making difficult trade-offs and crafting policies that incentivise biodiversity-friendly practices while penalising harmful ones.

Effective monitoring and reporting systems require substantial investment in technology, capacity building, and institutional frameworks. Countries need to develop standardised indicators and methodologies for assessing biodiversity and ensure that data is collected consistently over time. This may involve training personnel, establishing monitoring stations, and developing databases for storing and analysing biodiversity data. Reporting systems also need to be transparent and accessible to various stakeholders, including policymakers, researchers, and the public. Transparency fosters accountability and encourages broader participation in biodiversity conservation efforts.

State and Local Biodiversity Management

State- and local-level biodiversity conservation efforts play a crucial role in maintaining the ecological balance of specific regions. These efforts are often more targeted and adaptive, reflecting the unique needs and challenges of local environments.

State and regional conservation programmes are designed to address the specific ecological conditions of an area. For example, coastal states may focus on marine life preservation, while inland states might prioritise forest and freshwater ecosystems. Tailoring these programmes enables the implementation of appropriate measures that best suit the local flora and fauna. One notable example is California's Marine Life Protection Act, which establishes marine protected areas along the coast, ensuring sustainable fishing practices and protecting marine biodiversity. These localised approaches are essential for addressing the varied ecological needs across different regions and ensuring that conservation efforts are both effective and relevant to the particular environmental contexts they serve.

Community-based conservation efforts involve local populations in protecting their natural resources, making them key stakeholders in biodiversity conservation. By engaging communities in activities like reforestation, wildlife monitoring, and sustainable agriculture, these initiatives harness local knowledge and stewardship. The success of community-driven projects can be seen in the case of the Community Baboon Sanctuary in Belize, where local farmers have collectively agreed to protect the habitat of the black howler monkey. This collaboration has resulted in a thriving population of monkeys and enhanced awareness and appreciation of biodiversity among the community members. Engaging local populations not only enhances the effectiveness of conservation efforts but also ensures long-term sustainability by fostering a sense of ownership and responsibility towards natural resources.

Effective biodiversity management also requires collaboration between state and local governments, NGOs, and academia. Non-governmental organisations often provide technical expertise, funding, and manpower for conservation projects, while academic institutions contribute through research and scientific guidance. An exemplary model of such a partnership is the Florida Wildlife Corridor, a collaborative effort involving state agencies, NGOs like The Nature Conservancy, and universities. This initiative aims to connect fragmented habitats across the state, facilitating wildlife movement and genetic diversity. Collaborative efforts help integrate diverse perspectives and resources, leading to more comprehensive and successful conservation strategies. Moreover, these partnerships can leverage various strengths, such as the practical experience of NGOs, the policymaking authority of governments, and the research capabilities of academic institutions, creating a synergistic approach to biodiversity conservation.

Local biodiversity databases are invaluable tools in informing policy and action. Accurate and up-to-date data on species distribution, population trends, and habitat conditions enable policymakers to make informed decisions regarding conservation priorities. These databases also serve as critical resources for researchers and conservationists to monitor the effectiveness of ongoing efforts and identify emerging threats. The New York State Biodiversity Research Institute exemplifies this approach by maintaining comprehensive records of the state's biodiversity and aiding in habitat protection, species management, and the promotion of biodiversity-friendly land use practices. The importance of maintaining robust local biodiversity databases cannot be overstated, as they provide the empirical foundation necessary for evidence-based decision-making and adaptive management in conservation efforts.

Furthermore, state and local governments play pivotal roles in legislating and implementing conservation policies tailored to their regions' specific needs. Legal frameworks such as the Endangered Species Act at the state level or municipal ordinances dedicated to preserving green spaces can significantly impact local biodiversity. For example, the Texas Parks and Wildlife Department administers various programmes aimed at conserving native species and their habitats, from prairie chicken restoration projects to the preservation of rare plant species. Such legislative measures complement grassroots conservation efforts, providing structured support and legitimacy to biodiversity initiatives.

Education and outreach are also essential components of local conservation efforts. Informing the public about the importance of biodiversity and how they can contribute to its preservation fosters community support and participation. Programmes such as citizen science projects, educational workshops, and school-based environmental curricula engage individuals of all ages in conservation activities. For instance, Massachusetts' Biodiversity Project involves thousands of students in biodiversity monitoring, raising awareness and providing valuable data for conservationists. Educational initiatives empower communities to take proactive steps towards preserving their natural heritage and instilling a culture of environmental stewardship.

Moreover, economic incentives can be effective tools in promoting biodiversity conservation at the state and local levels. Programmes that offer financial rewards for sustainable practices, such as tax breaks for landowners who preserve natural habitats or subsidies for farmers adopting eco-friendly methods, encourage participation in conservation efforts. The Conservation Reserve Programme in the United States provides payments to farmers who convert environmentally sensitive agricultural land into natural habitats, benefiting both biodiversity and the agricultural economy. By aligning economic interests with conservation goals, such initiatives stimulate broader engagement in preserving biodiversity.

Research and innovation are fundamental to advancing local conservation efforts. Continuous scientific inquiry into species behaviour, ecosystem functions, and the impacts of human activities informs adaptive management strategies. Local research institutions and initiatives, such as the School of Field Studies in Queensland, Australia, which conducts field-based research in tropical rainforest ecosystems, contribute invaluable insights to local biodiversity management. Integrating cutting-edge research with traditional knowledge and contemporary conservation practices enhances the effectiveness and adaptability of biodiversity conservation efforts.

Finally, the involvement of indigenous communities and their traditional knowledge in biodiversity conservation efforts is of immense value. Indigenous peoples have managed their lands sustainably for generations, possessing extensive understanding of local ecosystems and species. Collaborations between state authorities and indigenous communities can result in more culturally sensitive and ecologically sound conservation practices. In Australia, the Indigenous Protected Areas programme empowers Aboriginal communities to manage and protect their lands, integrating traditional ecological knowledge with modern conservation techniques. Such inclusive approaches recognise the vital role of indigenous stewardship in biodiversity conservation and promote the integration of diverse knowledge systems in managing natural resources.

Role and Responsibility of Various Stakeholders

Government agencies play a crucial role in biodiversity conservation by creating and enforcing policies that protect ecosystems and species. These agencies develop national biodiversity strategies and action plans (NBSAPs) aligned with international commitments such as the Convention on Biological Diversity (CBD). They monitor compliance with environmental regulations, maintain protected areas, and implement laws to curb activities that threaten biodiversity.

For example, national parks and wildlife preserves managed by government bodies provide sanctuaries for endangered species. Effective policy implementation typically includes site-specific management plans tailored to local ecological conditions as well as broader frameworks that integrate biodiversity considerations into other sectors like agriculture and urban development. Agencies also invest in research programmes and educational campaigns to raise public awareness about the importance of biodiversity.

Non-governmental organisations (NGOs) are equally vital in advocating for biodiversity conservation and implementing various projects. NGOs often work on the ground, directly engaging with local communities to foster sustainable practices. Organisations like the World Wide Fund for Nature (WWF) and Conservation International have developed significant initiatives to restore habitats, protect endangered species, and reduce human impact on ecosystems.

One way NGOs contribute is by providing data sets and biodiversity indicators to track progress and guide policy decisions. The WWF and UNEP-WCMC, for instance, monitor the condition of the world's natural ecosystems through the "Living Planet Index." NGOs also engage in direct conservation actions, such as habitat restoration and species reintroduction projects. Their flexibility and often grassroots connections enable them to operate in areas where government intervention might be limited or less effective. Collaboration between NGOs and governments can amplify conservation efforts, ensuring policies are implemented successfully at multiple levels.

The private sector's involvement in biodiversity conservation has gained increasing attention as businesses recognise the economic and ethical imperatives of sustainable practices. Companies can support conservation through corporate social responsibility (CSR) initiatives, investments in sustainable supply chains, and partnerships with environmental groups. For example, many agricultural and forestry companies work to reduce their ecological footprint by adopting practices that preserve soil health, water quality, and local biodiversity.

Sustainable business models can also create new market opportunities. Eco-tourism, organic farming, and renewable energy are examples of industries that not only generate profits but also contribute positively to biodiversity conservation. Business associations and industry groups play an essential role in developing standards and guidelines that encourage members to adopt biodiversity-friendly practices. The Global Partnership for Business and Biodiversity, supported by the CBD Secretariat, promotes active and consistent collaboration between businesses and conservation stakeholders to achieve long-term environmental sustainability (Unit, 2007).

Indigenous communities hold a unique position in biodiversity conservation due to their traditional knowledge and deep-rooted connection to their lands. Indigenous peoples have managed their environments sustainably for generations, using practices that promote biodiversity and ecosystem health. Their knowledge systems often include detailed observations of plant and animal behaviour, climate patterns, and ecological relationships, making them invaluable partners in conservation efforts.

Many Indigenous communities participate in resource management programmes that blend traditional practices with modern conservation science. For example, traditional fire management techniques used by Indigenous rangers in Australia have not only enhanced biodiversity but also generated significant carbon credits and created meaningful employment (The Nature Conservancy, 2023). Such integrated approaches facilitate knowledge exchange and empower Indigenous peoples to assert their environmental and economic interests.

Additionally, Indigenous-led initiatives often emphasise the equitable distribution of benefits derived from conservation projects. Ensuring that these communities benefit economically and socially strengthens stewardship activities and leads to more durable outcomes for both people and nature. Programmes supporting Indigenous women and youth in leadership roles further enhance community capacity to manage and protect their natural resources effectively.

Maintaining Biodiversity Registers

Maintaining biodiversity registers plays a significant role in the conservation of our planet's myriad life forms. These registers document species and genetic diversity, acting as vital repositories of information that help scientists, policymakers, and environmentalists understand and protect Earth's biodiversity.

Biodiversity registers serve several critical purposes. Foremost among these is documenting species diversity, which involves cataloguing various species present in an ecosystem. This documentation provides fundamental data on the range of species within different habitats, thereby allowing conservationists to track changes over time. Additionally, these registers encompass genetic diversity, recording variations within species, which are crucial for understanding evolutionary processes and adaptability. The recorded data can inform conservation strategies aimed at maintaining genetic variability, which is essential for species to adapt to changing environments and resist diseases.

The methods for collecting and updating biodiversity data are diverse and multifaceted. Field surveys remain a cornerstone technique, where researchers physically observe and record species in specific locations. Collection of specimens for additional analysis and verification in laboratories is a common addition to these surveys. Citizen science initiatives also contribute significantly; everyday people report observations via apps and websites, supplementing professional data collection with valuable grassroots contributions. Remote sensing and geographic information systems (GIS) have revolutionised data collection, providing large-scale, high-resolution monitoring capabilities that can detect and analyse patterns in land use, habitat distribution, and ecosystem changes over time (Awais et al., 2023).

Moreover, molecular techniques such as DNA barcoding have become an indispensable tool. By analysing a small snippet of DNA, scientists can accurately identify species, even from small or degraded samples, thereby speeding up the identification process and improving accuracy. Advances in technology, particularly GIS and remote sensing, have significantly enhanced biodiversity management. Geographic Information Systems (GIS) facilitate the integration, analysis, and visualisation of spatial data from diverse sources (Tahri et al., 2021). They enable scientists to map species distributions, habitat extents, and other ecological variables over vast areas, thus providing a comprehensive overview of biodiversity hotspots and areas under threat. For example, GIS can reveal correlations between land use changes and species decline, guiding targeted conservation efforts.

Remote sensing technologies, including satellite imagery and aerial photography, provide consistent, up-to-date information on land cover and vegetation (Giri, 2016). These tools allow for timely detection of habitat loss, degradation, and fragmentation—key factors contributing to biodiversity loss. With this technology, ongoing changes in ecosystems can be monitored on a scale and with a frequency that traditional fieldwork cannot match. Combining these technologies offers detailed insights into the state of biodiversity and aids in making informed decisions about conservation priorities.

However, maintaining accurate and comprehensive biodiversity records comes with its own set of challenges. One primary challenge lies in the sheer volume and diversity of data required. Biodiversity encompasses millions of species across different habitats, each requiring specific data for effective monitoring. Ensuring consistent and standardised data collection methods across various regions and research groups is complex but essential for creating reliable registers. Data may come from disparate sources, including scientific research, government reports, and citizen science initiatives, each with varying levels of accuracy and detail. Harmonising this data into a coherent system requires meticulous quality control measures and cross-referencing.

Another significant challenge is funding. Comprehensive biodiversity monitoring is resource-intensive, requiring sustained financial support for field surveys, technology deployment, and data analysis. Limited funding often restricts the scope and frequency of data collection, leading to gaps in records that can hinder effective conservation planning. There is also the challenge of technological barriers. While advanced technologies like GIS and remote sensing offer powerful tools, they require technical expertise and infrastructure that may not be readily available in all regions, particularly in developing countries.

Another pressing issue is the dynamic nature of ecosystems. Biodiversity is not static; it continually evolves due to natural and human-induced factors. Climate change, invasive species, habitat destruction, and pollution can rapidly alter ecosystems, necessitating continuous updates to biodiversity registers. Keeping pace with these changes demands adaptive management strategies and prompt data processing and dissemination.

Human activities also complicate biodiversity records. Urbanisation, agricultural expansion, and deforestation significantly impact species and habitats, often resulting in rapid declines that are difficult to monitor continuously. Additionally, political and social factors can influence data accessibility and conservation efforts. In some regions, conflict or a lack of governance can impede data collection and sharing, exacerbating the challenge of maintaining comprehensive registers.

Ethical considerations must also be addressed. Biodiversity data often includes information about endangered species and sensitive habitats. Access to this information needs to be carefully controlled to prevent misuse, such as poaching or habitat destruction. Balancing transparency and security in data sharing is a delicate task that requires clear policies and cooperation among stakeholders.

Despite these challenges, the importance of maintaining comprehensive biodiversity registers cannot be overstated. They are invaluable tools for tracking and preserving the planet's biological wealth. Continued innovation in data collection methods, coupled with international collaboration and adequate funding, can help overcome current obstacles and ensure that biodiversity registers remain robust and relevant.

Final Insights

In this chapter, we have explored the various levels of biodiversity management, the roles of different stakeholders, and the methods for maintaining biodiversity registers. The chapter highlighted international efforts through treaties like the Convention on Biological Diversity (CBD) and the strategic role of organisations such as the United Nations Environment Programme (UNEP). National strategies were examined, emphasising the importance of National Biodiversity Strategies and Action Plans (NBSAPs), legal frameworks, cross-sectoral integration, and robust monitoring systems. At the state and local levels, targeted conservation efforts, community-based initiatives, and collaborative partnerships with NGOs and academia were discussed. Moreover, the role and responsibility of various stakeholders, including government agencies, NGOs, the private sector, and Indigenous communities, were detailed to provide a comprehensive understanding of how multi-level collaboration can effectively address biodiversity challenges.

The chapter also delved into the significance of maintaining biodiversity registers and the diverse methods employed in collecting and updating biodiversity data. From field surveys and citizen science initiatives to advanced molecular techniques and remote sensing technologies, these methods collectively contribute to creating accurate and comprehensive records essential for effective biodiversity conservation. Despite the challenges associated with funding, data consistency, and technological barriers, the continuous documentation of species diversity and genetic variability remains crucial for informed decision-making and adaptive management strategies. Ultimately, fostering international collaboration, innovation in data collection, and adequate resource allocation can help overcome these obstacles, ensuring the continued preservation of Earth's biodiversity.

Reference List

Convention on Biological Diversity. (2011). *CBD Home* . Cbd.int. https://www.cbd.int/

Kerry, R. G., Montalbo, F. J. P., Das, R., Patra, S., Mahapatra, G. P., Maurya, G. K., Nayak, V., Jena, A. B., Ukhurebor, K. E., Jena, R. C., Gouda, S., Majhi, S., & Rout, J. R. (2022, October 5). *An overview of remote monitoring methods in biodiversity conservation* . Environmental Science and Pollution Research. https://doi.org/10.1007/s11356-022-23242-y

Nizamani, M. M., Zhang, Q., Muhae-Ud-Din, G., Awais, M., & Wang, Y. (2023). *Application of GIS and remote-sensing technology in ecosystem services and biodiversity conservation* . *Deep Learning for Multimedia Processing Applications* , 284-321. https://doi.org/10.1201/9781032646268-12

Partnership - Center for Biodiversity Outcomes . (2024, June 20). Center for Biodiversity Outcomes; Center for Biodiversity Outcomes. https://globalfutures.asu.edu/center-for-biodiversity-outcomes/partnership/

The Nature Conservancy. (2023). *Partnering with Indigenous People and Local Communities* . The Nature Conservancy. https://www.nature.org/en-us/about-us/who-we-are/how-we-work/community-led-conservation/

Unit, B. (n.d.). *National Biodiversity Strategies and Action Plans (NBSAPs)* . Www.cbd.int. https://www.cbd.int/nbsap

UNEP. (2022, December 20). *COP15 ends with landmark biodiversity agreement* . UNEP. https://www.unep.org/news-and-stories/story/cop15-ends-landmark-biodiversity-agreement

Unit, B. (n.d.). *Post-COP10 NBSAPs (Aichi Biodiversity Target 17)* . Www.cbd.int. https://www.cbd.int/nbsap/about/latest

Unit, B. (2007, February 28). *Organizations and Stakeholders* . Www.cbd.int. https://www.cbd.int/cooperation/organizations.shtml

Dr. Anthonysamy David

White, R. M., Schmook, B., Calmé, S., Giordano, A. J., Hausser, Y., Kimmel, L., Lecuyer, L., Lucherini, M., Méndez-Medina, C., & Peña-Mondragón, J. L. (2023, June 1). *Facilitating biodiversity conservation through partnerships to achieve transformative outcomes* . Conservation Biology: The Journal of the Society for Conservation Biology. https://doi.org/10.1111/cobi.14057

Chapter 3

Biodiversity and Natural Resource Management

U nderstanding biodiversity's role in human society is essential for sustainable natural resource management. Biodiversity refers to the variety of life forms within different ecosystems, providing critical services such as air and water purification, climate regulation, and pollination. These services are integral to human health, food security, and overall well-being. Robust biodiversity also ensures ecosystems' resilience and adaptability, allowing them to recover from disruptions likc natural disasters and human activities. Hence, maintaining biodiversity is pivotal not only for ecological balance but also for sustaining the resources upon which human livelihoods depend.

This chapter will explore the multifaceted contributions of biodiversity to human society and the importance of sustainable conservation practices. It will detail how biodiversity supports ecological processes, enhances agricultural productivity, and contributes to medical discoveries. The chapter will also discuss strategies for promoting and preserving biodiversity, including habitat restoration, sustainable land use, and raising public awareness. Additionally, it will cover global policies and laws that aim to protect biodiversity and ensure the sustainable use of natural resources. Through these discussions, readers will gain a comprehensive understanding of the critical role biodiversity plays and the actions necessary to conserve it for future generations.

Importance of Biodiversity to Human Society

Biodiversity is a crucial component of our planet's well-being and human survival. The variety and variability among living organisms and their ecological complexes underpin many essential ecological services and resources that humans depend on daily. One of the most significant contributions of biodiversity is its provision of ecological services, including purifying the air and water, pollinating crops, decomposing waste, and regulating climate. These natural processes support food production, clean environments, and overall human health, ensuring our basic needs are met.

Moreover, biodiversity ensures the resilience and adaptability of ecosystems to environmental changes. Diverse ecosystems are better equipped to withstand and recover from disruptions such as climate change, natural disasters, and human activities. When an ecosystem has a variety of species, it can maintain functionality even if some species decline or disappear. For example, in agriculture, crop diversity can prevent severe impacts from pest invasions or diseases, thus safeguarding food security. Similarly, diverse marine ecosystems can better cope with overfishing and pollution, maintaining fish populations vital for global dietary needs.

In addition to ecological stability, biodiversity supports medicinal, agricultural, and economic benefits. Many modern pharmaceuticals are derived from plant and animal species. For instance, the anti-cancer drug Taxol comes from the Pacific yew tree, and artemisinin, an effective malaria treatment, is extracted from sweet wormwood. Without these species, critical medical treatments might never have been discovered, highlighting the role of biodiversity in healthcare advancements (Sandifer et al., 2015). Moreover, genetic diversity within crops and livestock contributes to agricultural resilience and productivity. Farmers rely on a range of species for pollination, pest control, and soil fertility, all of which underpin sustainable agricultural practices.

Economically, ecosystems rich in biodiversity offer substantial value. Natural areas foster tourism, which can be a major source of income for communities. National parks and wildlife reserves attract visitors, contributing to local economies while promoting conservation efforts. Furthermore, biodiversity provides raw materials for various industries, including timber, fibres, and biofuels, supporting livelihoods and economic development.

Cultural and aesthetic values also derive from biodiversity. Many cultures around the world have deep connections to nature, with spiritual, symbolic, and historical significance centred on various species and landscapes. Biodiversity enriches cultural heritage and identity, fostering a sense of place and community. Additionally, biodiverse environments enhance recreational experiences. Spending time in natural settings has been linked to improved mental health, increased life satisfaction, and reduced stress. Highly diverse environments, such as tropical rainforests or coral reefs, not only support myriad forms of life but also inspire awe and wonder, encouraging people to appreciate and protect these natural treasures (*Env iroAtlas Benefit Category: Biodiversity Conservation*, 2015).

Dr. Anthonysamy David

Promoting and Preserving Biodiversity

Establishing protected areas and wildlife reserves plays a key role in maintaining biodiversity. These designated regions provide safe habitats for flora and fauna, allowing ecosystems to function without the interference of human activities. Various countries have successfully implemented national parks, nature reserves, and marine sanctuaries to protect endangered species and their habitats. For instance, the establishment of Yellowstone National Park in the United States has provided a sanctuary for species like the grizzly bear and the American bison. By setting aside land specifically for conservation, governments can help preserve biodiversity hotspots, ensuring that these areas remain undisturbed and capable of supporting a variety of species.

Another crucial strategy for maintaining biodiversity is implementing habitat restoration and species reintroduction programmes. Habitat restoration involves restoring degraded landscapes, wetlands, forests, and other ecosystems to their natural state. This can include reforestation efforts, the removal of invasive species, and the rehabilitation of aquatic systems. For example, the reforestation projects in Costa Rica have significantly contributed to the recovery of tropical rainforests, promoting biodiversity and ecosystem services. Species reintroduction programmes involve reintroducing native species that have been extirpated from certain areas due to habitat destruction or other factors. The reintroduction of the grey wolf into Yellowstone National Park is a notable success story, resulting in improved ecosystem balance and increased biodiversity.

Encouraging sustainable land use and agricultural practices is another important measure to maintain biodiversity. Unsustainable agricultural methods, such as monoculture and excessive pesticide use, are major contributors to habitat destruction and biodiversity loss. Adopting eco-friendly farming techniques like organic farming, crop rotation, and integrated pest management can mitigate negative impacts on ecosystems. Furthermore, agroforestry, which combines agriculture and forestry, promotes habitat connectivity and supports diverse species. Supporting local, seasonal, and organically grown food products can also reduce the demand for environmentally harmful agricultural practices, thereby aiding biodiversity conservation.

Raising public awareness and education on biodiversity issues is vital for fostering a culture of conservation. Public education initiatives, such as workshops, school programmes, and nature centres, can inform individuals about the importance of biodiversity and the steps they can take to protect it. Educational outreach can also be achieved through media campaigns, popular articles, and interactive content that makes scientific research accessible to the general public. For instance, environmental documentaries like "Planet Earth" have played an essential role in raising awareness about global biodiversity and the need for conservation efforts. By empowering individuals with knowledge, we can inspire collective action towards preserving biodiversity.

In addition to these strategies, integrating biodiversity considerations into urban planning and policy-making is essential. Urban green spaces such as parks, gardens, and green roofs help mitigate the effects of urbanisation on ecosystems by providing habitats for various species. These green spaces also offer significant ecological benefits, including air purification, temperature regulation, and stormwater management. Cities like Singapore have effectively incorporated extensive green infrastructure, enhancing biodiversity while improving the quality of urban life. Policies that mandate the inclusion of green spaces in urban development plans can significantly contribute to biodiversity conservation.

Governments and local authorities should also adopt policies that protect critical habitats and develop plans to expand or replicate these areas. Zoning laws and ordinances can be designed to restrict developments near sensitive ecosystems, ensuring that land use decisions prioritise conservation. For example, buffer zones around wetlands and forests can prevent habitat fragmentation and degradation. Additionally, conducting habitat impact assessments for new developments can help identify potential threats to biodiversity and implement measures to mitigate these impacts. Allowing landowners to sell their development rights to local governments for permanent land protection, known as the transfer or purchase of development rights, is another effective strategy. This not only safeguards habitats but also compensates landowners, making conservation economically viable.

Supporting private-sector and residential habitat restoration projects can further enhance biodiversity. Governments can provide incentives for native landscaping and conservation efforts on both public and private properties. A formal commitment to using native plants in public landscaping projects can promote ecological balance and support native species. Conservation organisations often collaborate with local communities and volunteers to implement habitat restoration projects, generating social, economic, and environmental benefits for everyone involved.

Successful restoration efforts result in increased biodiversity, improved habitat quality, and the recovery of threatened species.

Monitoring and maintenance are critical components of any conservation strategy. After implementing habitat restoration and species reintroduction programmes, continuous monitoring allows conservationists to track progress and adjust management practices as necessary. Regular maintenance activities, such as controlling invasive species and maintaining infrastructure, ensure the long-term success of restoration projects. The involvement of local communities in monitoring efforts can foster a sense of stewardship and responsibility towards the environment.

Adopting controls on invasive species is vital for maintaining biodiversity, as invasive species can outcompete native ones and disrupt ecosystems. Local governments can monitor known locations of invasive plants and implement management plans to mitigate their impact (Adaptation Strategies for Maintaining Biodiversity, n.d.). Education programmes aimed at raising awareness about invasive species can also be effective in preventing their spread.

Finally, supporting conservation organisations through financial contributions, volunteer work, or partnerships can amplify their efforts to protect wildlife habitats. These organisations often spearhead research, restoration projects, and advocacy efforts, playing a crucial role in biodiversity conservation (*3 Ways to Conserve Wildlife Habitats | GVI*, n.d.). Participating in citizen science projects, where individuals contribute data and observations, can also support conservation research and increase public engagement with biodiversity issues.

Human Response to Biodiversity Conservation

Participating in global and local conservation initiatives is a fundamental proactive measure to preserve biodiversity. Engaging in such initiatives allows individuals and communities to contribute directly to environmental protection efforts. Globally, organisations like the World Wildlife Fund (WWF) and the International Union for Conservation of Nature (IUCN) lead extensive projects to conserve natural habitats, protect endangered species, and restore ecological balance. Locally, community-based programmes play a pivotal role in conserving regional biodiversity. These programmes can include activities like tree planting, clean-up drives, and citizen science projects that record local wildlife and monitor ecosystems.

Participating in these initiatives not only promotes immediate environmental benefits but also fosters a sense of stewardship among participants. It helps individuals understand their impact on local and global ecosystems, encouraging more sustainable behaviours over time. Additionally, it enables stakeholders to share knowledge, technology, and strategies across borders, enhancing the overall effectiveness of conservation efforts.

Adopting eco-friendly lifestyles and reducing carbon footprints are critical steps towards sustainable living and biodiversity preservation. Eco-friendly lifestyles encompass various practices, such as minimising waste, recycling, using energy-efficient appliances, and choosing sustainable products. Reducing one's carbon footprint involves adopting renewable energy sources, using public transportation, cycling or walking instead of driving, and consuming less meat and dairy, which have high carbon emissions associated with production.

These lifestyle changes have significant positive impacts on biodiversity by mitigating climate change, reducing pollution, and conserving natural resources. For example, reducing plastic usage decreases plastic pollution in oceans, benefiting marine life. Similarly, choosing locally-sourced, organic food reduces the need for pesticide use, which can be harmful to pollinators like bees and butterflies. While individual actions may seem small, collectively, they drive substantial change in reducing human-induced pressures on ecosystems.

Supporting policies and regulations aimed at protecting biodiversity is another essential proactive measure. Policies provide a framework for managing and safeguarding natural resources, ensuring that economic development does not come at the expense of environmental health. Supporting policies can be done by voting for leaders committed to environmental protection, advocating for stronger environmental laws, and participating in public consultations on proposed regulations.

Examples of effective policies include laws that restrict deforestation, regulate wildlife trade, and mandate the creation of protected areas. For instance, the European Union's Natura 2000 network protects numerous habitats and species across member states, demonstrating how policy can enforce conservation at a large scale. Moreover, international agreements such as the Convention on Biological Diversity (CBD) set goals for preserving biodiversity and promoting sustainable use of its components, guiding national policies globally.

Engaging in community-based conservation efforts addresses the unique needs and circumstances of local environments while empowering communities to manage their natural resources sustainably. Community-based conservation recognises the importance of involving local people who live in and depend on biodiversity for their livelihoods. As highlighted in recent studies, this approach supports both livelihoods and biodiversity, reinforcing local and Indigenous values, cultures, and institutions (Esmail et al., 2023).

Community-based projects often include activities like creating community-managed forests, establishing conservation areas, and developing eco-tourism ventures. For example, in the Amazon rainforest, many Indigenous communities manage their territories to protect the forest from illegal logging and mining activities. Such efforts ensure that conservation measures are culturally appropriate and economically beneficial, fostering long-term sustainability.

Furthermore, community-based conservation offers opportunities to address cross-cutting global challenges such as climate change, poverty, and food security. By integrating traditional knowledge with scientific practices, these initiatives enhance the resilience of ecosystems and improve the well-being of local populations (Esmail et al., 2023). The success of these efforts depends on genuine partnerships between local communities, governments, NGOs, and other stakeholders, ensuring that conservation goals align with community needs.

Global Policies and Laws on Biodiversity

The Convention on Biological Diversity (CBD) serves as a comprehensive framework aimed at promoting sustainable practices for the conservation and sustainable use of biodiversity. Adopted at the Earth Summit in 1992, the CBD has three primary objectives: the conservation of biological diversity, the sustainable use of its components, and the fair and equitable sharing of benefits arising from genetic resources. These objectives underscore the importance of biodiversity in maintaining ecosystem health, economic development, and human well-being. By providing a global platform for countries to collaborate, the CBD encourages the implementation of national strategies to conserve and sustainably manage biological diversity (Convention on Biological Diversity, 2011).

The regulation of wildlife trade and protection of endangered species is another critical component in preserving biodiversity. The Convention on International Trade in Endangered Species of Wild Fauna and Flora (CITES) regulates international trade in specimens of wild animals and plants to ensure that their survival in the wild is not threatened. CITES classifies species into three appendices based on their level of risk. Appendix I includes species threatened with extinction, prohibiting commercial trade except under exceptional circumstances. Appendix II covers species that are not necessarily threatened with extinction but may become so without trade controls, allowing regulated trade if certain conditions are met. Appendix III contains species protected in at least one country which has requested assistance in controlling trade. This tiered system enables CITES to provide appropriate levels of protection and promote international cooperation (Fisheries, 2020).

Marine and terrestrial ecosystem conservation agreements play an essential role in safeguarding biodiversity. For example, the United Nations Convention on the Law of the Sea (UNCLOS) outlines nations' rights and responsibilities regarding ocean resources, promoting sustainable management and conservation of marine ecosystems. Specific agreements, such as the recent Kunming-Montreal Global Biodiversity Framework, emphasise halting and reversing biodiversity loss by 2030. The framework sets ambitious targets for protecting marine and terrestrial habitats, aiming to restore degraded ecosystems and increase the area of protected land and sea.

Cross-border cooperation is vital for effective biodiversity conservation. National legislation often provides the foundation for conservation efforts, yet many ecological challenges transcend borders and require international collaboration. Bilateral and multilateral treaties facilitate coordinated actions, such as the management of shared water bodies or migratory species. The European Union's Natura 2000 network exemplifies a successful regional approach, establishing a coherent ecological network across member states to protect vulnerable species and habitats within the EU.

Sustainable Use of Natural Resources

Implementing sustainable harvesting and fishing practices is fundamental for prudent resource management. Sustainable harvesting involves methods that allow forests and other natural resources to regenerate, ensuring longevity and biodiversity. For instance, selective logging, which focuses on removing only specific trees, helps maintain the forest structure and promotes the growth of new vegetation. It reduces soil erosion and protects water quality in adjacent streams and rivers. Similarly, the adoption of reduced-impact logging techniques minimises damage to the surrounding ecosystem during timber extraction.

In the context of fisheries, sustainable fishing practices are essential to prevent overfishing and ensure the long-term viability of fish populations. This includes setting catch limits based on scientific assessments of fish stocks, employing fishing gear that minimises bycatch, and establishing marine protected areas where fishing is restricted or prohibited. For example, using fish traps with escape mechanisms allows non-target species and juvenile fish to escape, reducing unnecessary catches and supporting the sustainability of multiple species within the ecosystem. Community-based management approaches, where local fishers participate in decision-making processes, have also proven successful in promoting sustainable use of marine resources (Karjalainen et al., 2005).

Promoting renewable energy sources and reducing resource depletion are crucial steps towards sustainable resource management. The transition from fossil fuels to renewable energy sources such as wind, solar, and hydroelectric power not only decreases greenhouse gas emissions but also alleviates pressure on finite natural resources. For example, solar panels installed on rooftops can harness sunlight to generate electricity, reducing reliance on coal and natural gas. Wind turbines contribute to clean energy production without emitting pollutants or depleting raw materials. Moreover, advancements in battery storage technology enable more efficient use of renewable energy, ensuring a steady supply even when natural conditions fluctuate.

Reducing resource depletion also involves enhancing energy efficiency across various sectors. Implementing energy-saving technologies in industrial processes, adopting energy-efficient appliances in households, and improving building insulation are effective measures. For instance, replacing incandescent bulbs with LED lights significantly lowers electricity consumption while providing the same level of illumination. Retrofitting existing infrastructure with modern, energy-efficient systems can substantially reduce overall energy demand, thereby conserving natural resources and mitigating environmental impacts.

Protecting indigenous people's rights and traditional knowledge is integral to sustainable resource management. Indigenous communities often possess extensive knowledge of their local ecosystems, developed over generations of close interaction with nature. Recognising and respecting these rights not only safeguards their cultural heritage but also enriches conservation efforts with valuable insights. For example, traditional fire management practices used by indigenous Australians involve controlled burns that reduce fuel loads and enhance biodiversity. Such practices can complement modern scientific approaches, leading to more effective and culturally resonant conservation strategies.

Furthermore, granting legal recognition to indigenous land rights is vital for empowering these communities and preventing exploitation by external entities. When indigenous peoples have secure land tenure, they are better positioned to manage their resources sustainably and resist environmentally destructive activities such as illegal logging, mining, and agricultural expansion. Collaborative projects that integrate indigenous knowledge with contemporary conservation science can yield innovative solutions tailored to specific ecological contexts, benefiting both local communities and global biodiversity.

Reviewing commission reports and patents to ensure sustainability is another key aspect of resource management. Regularly assessing the environmental impact of various industries and innovations helps identify potential threats and opportunities for improvement. Commission reports, like those produced by environmental agencies and research institutions, provide critical data on resource usage trends, ecological health, and the effectiveness of current management practices. By analysing these reports, policymakers can make informed decisions to adjust regulations, allocate resources, and promote sustainable development initiatives.

Patents related to new technologies and industrial processes should also be scrutinised for their environmental implications. Innovations that offer substantial benefits in terms of efficiency, waste reduction, or resource conservation should be encouraged and supported. For instance, developments in biodegradable packaging materials can significantly decrease plastic pollution. However, a thorough evaluation is necessary to ensure that these technologies do not introduce unforeseen adverse effects. Transparent and stringent patent review processes can help balance technological progress with ecological responsibility, fostering innovations that align with sustainability goals.

Summary and Reflections

In this chapter, we have explored the critical importance of biodiversity to human society and outlined various strategies for its conservation. Biodiversity not only provides essential ecological services such as air and water purification, pollination, and climate regulation but also ensures the resilience and adaptability of ecosystems. This chapter has highlighted how diverse ecosystems can better withstand environmental disruptions and support agricultural productivity, medicinal advancements, and economic stability. Understanding and appreciating these benefits are essential for fostering a commitment to preserving biodiversity.

We have also examined practical measures to promote and preserve biodiversity, including establishing protected areas, implementing habitat restoration programmes, and promoting sustainable land use practices. Raising public awareness and integrating biodiversity considerations into urban planning are vital steps that enhance conservation efforts. Additionally, supporting policies and community-based initiatives, along with encouraging eco-friendly lifestyles, contribute significantly to long-term sustainability. Overall, by understanding the multifaceted value of biodiversity and actively participating in its conservation, human society can secure a healthier and more resilient future.

Reference List

3 Ways to Conserve Wildlife Habitats | GVI . (n.d.). Www.gviusa.com. https://www.gviusa.com/blog/smb-3-ways-to-conserve-wildlife-habitats-2/

Adaptation strategies for maintaining biodiversity . (n.d.). Environmental Resilience Institute. https://eri.iu.edu/erit/strategies/maintaining-biodiversity.html

Bansard, J., & Schroder, M. (2021, April 15). *The Sustainable Use of Natural Resources: The Governance Challenge* . International Institute for Sustainable Development. https://www.iisd.org/articles/deep-dive/sustainable-use-natural-resources-governance-challenge

C40 Knowledge Community . (2024). C40knowledgehub.org. https:// www.c40knowledgehub.org/s/article/How-to-enhance-restore-and-protect-biodiversity-in-your-city

Convention on Biological Diversity. (2011). *CBD Home* . Cbd.int. https://www.cbd.int/

Esmail, N., McPherson, J. M., Abulu, L., Amend, T., Amit, R., Bhatia, S., Bikaba, D., Brichieri-Colombi, T. A., Brown, J., Buschman, V., Fabinyi, M., Farhadinia, M., Ghayoumi, R., Hay-Edie, T., Horigue, V., Jungblut, V., Jupiter, S., Keane, A., Macdonald, D. W., & Mahajan, S. L. (2023, March 17). *What's on the horizon for community-based conservation? Emerging threats and opportunities* . Trends in Ecology and Evolution. https://doi.org/ 10.1016/j.tree.2023.02.008

EnviroAtlas Benefit Category: Biodiversity Conservation . (2015, April 24). US EPA. https://www.epa.gov/enviroatlas/enviroatlas-benefit-category-biodiversity-conservation

Fisheries, N. (2020, June 24). *Convention on International Trade in Endangered Species of Wild Fauna and Flora NOAA Fisheries* . NOAA. https://www.fisheries.noaa.gov/national/international-affairs/convention-international-trade-endangered-species-wild-fauna-and

Karjalainen, J., & Marjomäki, T. J. (2005). *Sustainability in fisheries management* . *ResearchGate* . Retrieved from https://www.researchgate.net/publication/236942810_Sustainability_in_fisheries_management

Sandifer, P. A., Sutton-Grier, A. E., & Ward, B. P. (2015, April). *Exploring connections among nature, biodiversity, ecosystem services, and human health and well-being: Opportunities to enhance health and biodiversity conservation* . Ecosystem Services. https://doi.org/10.1016/j.ecoser.2014.12.007

Chapter 4

Applied Biodiversity

E xploring the implementation and impact of biodiversity projects at various levels reveals a critical intersection between ecological health and sustainable human practices. Applied biodiversity encompasses efforts to preserve species diversity, promote sustainable resource use, mitigate climate change impacts, and enhance habitat connectivity. These projects are essential for maintaining ecosystem resilience and ensuring that natural resources can support both current and future generations.

This chapter delves into the various goals and actions associated with applied biodiversity projects. It covers the preservation and enhancement of species diversity as fundamental objectives, illustrating how these efforts stabilise ecosystems. Additionally, it examines sustainable land and resource use practices critical for mitigating environmental degradation. The chapter also addresses the challenges posed by climate change and outlines strategies for creating resilient ecosystems through habitat restoration and conservation. Furthermore, it discusses the importance of improving habitat connectivity to support wildlife migration, thus maintaining genetic diversity and adaptability within species. By exploring these multifaceted approaches, the chapter provides a comprehensive overview of applied biodiversity initiatives and their significance in global conservation efforts.

Goals of Applied Biodiversity Projects

Applied biodiversity projects aim to preserve and enhance species diversity, promote sustainable resource use, mitigate climate change impacts, and improve habitat connectivity. These objectives are fundamental to ensuring the resilience of ecosystems and the services they provide.

Preserving and enhancing species diversity in ecosystems is a critical goal of applied biodiversity projects. Biodiversity ensures ecosystem stability and productivity. Diverse ecosystems are better able to withstand environmental stressors such as disease, climate change, and invasive species. For example, maintaining a variety of plant species can reduce the likelihood of pest outbreaks and promote pollination. Projects that focus on preserving habitats like forests, wetlands, and coral reefs help protect countless species from extinction. Conservation efforts often include establishing protected areas, wildlife reserves, and national parks, which serve as refuges for endangered species. By protecting these areas, we also safeguard genetic diversity, which is crucial for adaptation and evolution.

Promoting sustainable land and resource use is another essential aim. Unsustainable practices, such as deforestation, overfishing, and industrial agriculture, deplete natural resources and degrade habitats. Sustainable land use practices ensure that natural resources are used in a way that meets current needs without compromising future generations' ability to meet theirs. Agroforestry, for instance, integrates agricultural and forestry practices to create more diverse, productive, profitable, and sustainable land-use systems. This approach not only enhances soil fertility and crop yields but also provides habitat for various species. Sustainable fisheries management, which includes setting catch limits and protecting spawning grounds, helps maintain fish populations and marine biodiversity. Additionally, promoting the use of renewable energy sources reduces dependence on fossil fuels, thus lessening habitat destruction from mining and drilling activities.

Mitigating the impacts of climate change on biodiversity is imperative. Climate change poses significant threats to ecosystems by altering temperature and precipitation patterns, causing sea levels to rise, and increasing the frequency of extreme weather events. Species may struggle to adapt to these rapid changes, leading to shifts in distribution or even extinction. Applied biodiversity projects aim to create resilient ecosystems that can endure climate change effects. For example, restoring coastal wetlands can protect shorelines from storm surges and provide critical habitats for migratory birds and fish. Reforestation projects sequester carbon, reducing greenhouse gas concentrations in the atmosphere. According to Weiskopf (Weiskopf, 2020), proactive and flexible adaptation strategies are necessary for natural resource managers to minimise long-term costs and enhance ecosystem resilience. By integrating climate action with biodiversity conservation, projects can address both challenges simultaneously, creating co-benefits.

Improving habitat connectivity to support wildlife migration is vital for maintaining biodiversity. Many species need to move between habitats to find food, mates, and suitable living conditions. Fragmented landscapes can hinder these movements, isolating populations and reducing genetic diversity. Wildlife corridors, which link fragmented habitats, allow animals to move freely across the landscape. These corridors can be established through the restoration of degraded areas or by creating new pathways, such as green bridges over highways. In North America, for example, wildlife crossings have been implemented to reduce vehicle collisions and facilitate the movement of large mammals like deer and elk. Enhancing connectivity also helps species respond to climate change by allowing them to migrate to more suitable environments as conditions shift. According to Newell et al. (2022), maintaining green spaces can enhance biodiversity and contribute to climate mitigation and adaptation.

Actions Taken by Various Stakeholders

Government initiatives play a crucial role in establishing and managing protected areas to safeguard biodiversity. Governments can designate regions as national parks, wildlife reserves, or marine protected areas (MPAs) to ensure the long-term conservation of ecosystems. For instance, the creation of Yellowstone National Park in the United States set a precedent for worldwide conservation efforts. These protected areas serve as sanctuaries for endangered species, mitigate habitat destruction, and maintain ecological balance. Government policies also include regulatory frameworks that restrict activities like logging, mining, and deforestation within these regions, ensuring the habitats remain undisturbed.

NGOs contribute significantly to community-based conservation programmes. They bridge the gap between local communities and broader conservation goals by involving residents in protecting their natural surroundings. Projects such as reforestation, anti-poaching patrols, and sustainable agriculture practices are often spearheaded by NGOs with active community participation. For example, the Maasai Wilderness Conservation Trust works with the Maasai community in Kenya to protect wildlife and promote sustainable livelihoods. Additionally, NGOs often undertake educational campaigns to raise awareness about environmental issues and encourage conservation behaviour among the public. According to Saghira (2024), NGOs have made significant contributions through advocacy and public engagement in conservation efforts.

The corporate sector also plays a pivotal role in biodiversity conservation through corporate social responsibility (CSR) initiatives. Businesses can implement sustainable practices that reduce their ecological footprint while supporting conservation projects. Companies might fund reforestation efforts, clean-up drives, or wildlife protection programmes. For example, Patagonia, a global outdoor clothing brand, donates a portion of its profits to environmental preservation projects and has taken steps to make its supply chain more sustainable. Through CSR, corporations not only contribute financially but also promote environmental stewardship within their industry and among consumers.

Academic and research institutions are instrumental in advancing biodiversity conservation strategies through their studies and innovations. Universities and research centres conduct essential research on species behaviour, ecosystem dynamics, and the impacts of climate change on biodiversity. These findings contribute to evidence-based conservation practices. Research institutions often collaborate with governments and NGOs to develop technologies and methodologies for monitoring and preserving biodiversity. For instance, satellite tracking of wildlife movements helps in understanding migration patterns and designing effective conservation corridors. Furthermore, academic publications disseminate knowledge globally, informing policy decisions and conservation strategies.

One notable example of government-led conservation is the Amazon Region Protected Areas (ARPA) Programme in Brazil. This initiative aims to protect the rich biodiversity of the Amazon rainforest by creating and maintaining extensive protected areas. The programme collaborates with various stakeholders, including indigenous communities, to manage and monitor these regions effectively. Similarly, Costa Rica's Payment for Environmental Services (PES) programme incentivizes landowners to conserve forests and undertake reforestation, showcasing a successful model of government intervention in biodiversity conservation.

NGOs like the World Wildlife Fund (WWF) and Conservation International have been at the forefront of numerous community-based projects. WWF's project in Nepal's Terai Arc Landscape engages local communities in tiger conservation efforts, leading to a significant increase in the tiger population. Similarly, Conservation International's work with the Kayapo people in the Brazilian Amazon protects millions of acres of rainforest from deforestation and illegal logging. These examples highlight how NGOs leverage local knowledge and community involvement to achieve conservation success.

In the corporate realm, Unilever's Sustainable Living Plan exemplifies how businesses can integrate sustainability into their operations. The company aims to halve its environmental footprint while doubling its business size. Initiatives include sourcing raw materials sustainably, reducing greenhouse gas emissions, and improving water efficiency. Such efforts demonstrate that corporate involvement in conservation is not only beneficial for biodiversity but also enhances brand reputation and consumer trust.

Academic institutions such as the Smithsonian Institution and the University of Cambridge lead groundbreaking research in biodiversity conservation. The Smithsonian's ForestGEO network monitors forests globally to understand changes in biodiversity and inform conservation policies. The University of Cambridge's Conservation Research Institute collaborates with governments and NGOs to apply scientific findings to real-world conservation challenges. Through research and innovation, academic institutions provide the scientific backbone necessary for effective biodiversity management.

Local-level implementation

Community involvement in monitoring and protecting local ecosystems plays a significant role in biodiversity conservation at the local level. Residents who are knowledgeable about their environment are more likely to notice changes, such as the introduction of invasive species or changes in water quality, that could indicate larger ecological issues. For instance, community science projects can engage residents in collecting data on local wildlife populations and water quality, contributing valuable information that can be used by scientists and policymakers. This grassroots approach not only provides essential data but also fosters a sense of stewardship and connectivity among community members.

Localised restoration projects, such as reforestation and wetland rehabilitation, are another vital component of applying biodiversity initiatives locally. Reforestation efforts can combat deforestation's adverse effects, such as soil erosion and habitat loss. Wetland rehabilitation restores these crucial ecosystems, known for their biodiversity and natural water filtration capacities. An example is the planting of native trees and plants in deforested areas to restore natural habitats and improve carbon sequestration. Local efforts in these activities typically involve volunteer groups, schools, and local government bodies working together to achieve common environmental goals. These projects often transform degraded areas into vibrant ecosystems that provide numerous ecological services and enhance local biodiversity.

The establishment of urban green spaces is essential for enhancing biodiversity within city limits. Urban areas with parks, community gardens, and green roofs contribute significantly to local biodiversity. These green spaces act as mini-habitats for various plant and animal species, and they help mitigate urban heat island effects while improving air quality. For instance, transforming vacant lots into community gardens can provide sanctuaries for pollinators like bees and butterflies, contributing to overall ecosystem diversity.

Moreover, green spaces offer residents recreational areas that enhance physical and mental well-being, creating a healthy environment for both humans and wildlife.

Integrating traditional knowledge with modern conservation practices allows for a more holistic approach to biodiversity conservation. Indigenous and local communities often possess extensive knowledge about their ecosystems, including sustainable land management techniques and species-specific behaviours. By combining this traditional knowledge with contemporary scientific methods, conservation strategies can be more effective and culturally relevant. For example, using traditional fire management practices can promote forest health and reduce the risk of catastrophic wildfires. Additionally, involving local communities in conservation planning ensures that projects are respectful of cultural values and are more likely to succeed in the long term.

Engaging the community in monitoring and protecting local ecosystems requires education and capacity-building initiatives. Workshops, training sessions, and educational outreach programmes can equip residents with the skills needed to participate effectively in biodiversity projects. Educational institutions and NGOs can play a pivotal role in this by developing curricula focused on local biodiversity and practical conservation skills. Providing resources such as identification guides, monitoring equipment, and access to online databases can further empower individuals and groups to take action.

Localised restoration projects often face challenges such as securing funding, gaining community support, and navigating regulatory frameworks. Overcoming these obstacles requires strategic planning and collaboration among stakeholders. Grant writing and fundraising campaigns can generate financial support for restoration initiatives. Engaging the community through awareness campaigns and public meetings can build the necessary support base. Collaboration with local authorities and compliance with environmental regulations ensure that projects are legally sound and recognised by official entities.

Dr. Anthonysamy David

Urban green spaces need to be thoughtfully designed and maintained to maximise their biodiversity benefits. Selecting native plant species that provide food and shelter for local wildlife is crucial. Incorporating features such as ponds, birdhouses, and insect hotels can create diverse habitats within green spaces. Regular maintenance, such as weeding, watering, and removing litter, ensures these areas remain viable for wildlife. Community involvement in the creation and upkeep of urban green spaces fosters a sense of ownership and responsibility.

The integration of traditional knowledge in modern conservation efforts is facilitated through partnerships with indigenous and local communities. Respecting intellectual property rights and ensuring equitable benefit-sharing are key considerations in these collaborations. Participatory approaches that involve community members in decision-making processes enhance the relevance and acceptance of conservation initiatives. Documenting and disseminating successful case studies of traditional knowledge integration can inspire other communities to adopt similar practices.

National-Level Implementation

National policies and legislation play a crucial role in biodiversity conservation efforts at the national level. Countries often enact comprehensive biodiversity policies that set the framework for conservation activities, including laws aimed at protecting endangered species, regulating land use, and maintaining ecological balance. These policies often mandate environmental impact assessments for development projects, ensuring that potential harms to ecosystems is minimised. For example, the Endangered Species Act (ESA) in the United States mandates federal agencies to protect and recover imperilled species and the ecosystems upon which they depend.

Effective implementation of these policies requires robust legal frameworks and capable enforcement bodies. This includes the establishment of national parks, reserves, and protected areas designated by law to conserve biodiversity hotspots. Additionally, nations frequently update their environmental laws to adapt to new challenges posed by climate change, pollution, and urbanisation. National legislation thus serves as the backbone for implementing large-scale biodiversity conservation initiatives.

Large-scale habitat corridors are integral in facilitating species movement across regions, helping to maintain genetic diversity and ecosystem resilience. These corridors connect isolated habitats, allowing wildlife to migrate, forage, and reproduce without the barriers imposed by human development. In the United States, the establishment of wildlife corridors is often supported by bipartisan efforts, recognizing that habitat connectivity is essential for species like Pronghorn, big horn, and Mule Deer. The Wildlife Movement Through Partnerships Act, for instance, aims to solidify the intent of promoting public-private partnerships in conservation and focuses on migratory big game (Padilla, Zinke, and Beyer

Announce Bipartisan Bill to Strengthen Habitat Connectivity and Migration Corridors, Senator Alex Padilla, 2024).

Creating such corridors involves strategic planning and collaboration among various stakeholders, including government agencies, non-profit organisations, and private landowners. Successful examples include the Yellowstone to Yukon Conservation Initiative, which spans over 2,000 miles and ensures that species can move freely across this vast area. Large-scale habitat corridors not only benefit wildlife but also contribute to ecosystem services that humans depend on, such as water purification and climate regulation.

Funding and grants at the national level are pivotal in driving biodiversity research and conservation projects. Governments allocate significant financial resources to support scientific studies, fieldwork, and the implementation of conservation strategies. These funds are often distributed through competitive grant programmes, encouraging innovation and the development of effective conservation practices. The Bipartisan

Infrastructure Law's Wildlife Crossings Pilot Programme allocates $350 million over five years to states and other eligible applicants interested in constructing wildlife crossings, thus promoting biodiversity while reducing wildlife-vehicle collisions (Habitat Connectivity: A Win for Biodiversity, n.d.).

In addition to direct funding, governments often provide tax incentives and subsidies to encourage private sector investments in biodiversity projects. Public-private partnerships are also common, where corporate entities collaborate with governments and NGOs to fund and implement conservation initiatives. These collaborations enhance resource mobilisation, ensuring sustained funding for long-term projects. The provision of technical assistance and capacity-building programmes further supports local entities in effectively utilising funds.

Collaboration between federal agencies and local governments is essential to achieving conservation goals. Federal agencies typically set overarching conservation objectives and provide the necessary resources and expertise, while local governments implement these initiatives on the ground. This multi-level approach ensures that conservation strategies are tailored to the specific needs of different regions and communities. The collaborative effort is exemplified by the Theodore Roosevelt Conservation Partnership, which emphasises locally driven projects to restore and conserve critical migratory routes and habitats (Padilla, Zinke, and Beyer Announce Bipartisan Bill to Strengthen Habitat Connectivity and Migration Corridors, Senator Alex Padilla, 2024).

Inter-agency cooperation enhances the effectiveness of biodiversity projects by pooling knowledge and resources. For instance, the U.S. Geological Survey corridor mapping team collaborates with state and tribal agencies to accurately map wildlife movement areas. This data-driven approach informs policy decisions and helps target conservation efforts where they are most needed. The involvement of local governments ensures community engagement and the incorporation of local knowledge into conservation plans, making these initiatives more sustainable and culturally relevant.

Global-Level Implementation

Evaluating global efforts and collaboration in biodiversity initiatives reveals an intricate network of treaties, programmes, funding mechanisms, and research collaborations designed to address the myriad challenges of biodiversity loss. These collective actions are instrumental in promoting conservation and sustainable use of biological resources on local, national, and international scales.

One of the cornerstones of global biodiversity efforts are international treaties and agreements like the Convention on Biological Diversity (CBD). The CBD, which came into force in 1993, aims to conserve biological diversity, ensure the sustainable use of its components, and guarantee the equitable sharing of benefits arising from the utilisation of genetic resources. This comprehensive framework addresses ecosystems, species, and genetic resources globally. Moreover, it paved the way for subsequent agreements such as the Nagoya Protocol on Access and Benefit- Sharing and the Cartagena Protocol on Biosafety, both of which provide specific operational guidelines and frameworks to enhance biodiversity conservation and sustainable use (Unit, 2017).

Cross-border conservation programmes play a pivotal role in protecting migratory species that traverse national boundaries. Such species are often vulnerable due to their extensive habitat requirements and the diverse threats they face during migration. The Convention on the Conservation of Migratory Species of Wild Animals (CMS), also known as the Bonn Convention, exemplifies these collaborative efforts. Established with the mission to conserve terrestrial, marine, and avian migratory species throughout their range, CMS facilitates cooperation among countries to protect habitats, mitigate threats, and promote sustainable practices. By providing strict protection measures for endangered species, fostering regional multilateral agreements, and encouraging cooperative research, the CMS enhances the survival prospects of migratory species (Unit, 2017).

Global funding mechanisms are another critical aspect of biodiversity initiatives. The Global Environment Facility (GEF) stands out as a vital financial resource for developing countries undertaking environmental projects. Since its establishment, GEF has provided billions of dollars in grants for biodiversity conservation, along with substantial co-financing from various partners. These funds support projects that combat biodiversity loss, promote sustainable land management, and protect ecosystems. By leveraging financial resources, GEF enables countries to implement large-scale conservation projects, develop national biodiversity strategies, and integrate biodiversity considerations into broader policy frameworks.

Multinational research collaborations are essential to addressing biodiversity loss and enhancing ecosystem services. Research institutions, universities, and environmental organisations across different countries work together to collect data, conduct studies, and develop innovative solutions. These collaborations help identify trends in biodiversity loss, understand underlying causes, and formulate effective conservation strategies. For instance, projects studying coral reef health, forest dynamics, or pollinator populations benefit significantly from shared resources, expertise, and technology. By pooling knowledge and efforts, these multinational collaborations drive advancements in conservation science and inform policy decisions at various levels.

The importance of these initiatives can be further broken down by examining the goals and achievements of specific conventions. For example, the Ramsar Convention on Wetlands, established in 1971, focusses on the conservation and wise use of wetlands through local, regional, and national actions. Wetlands are crucial ecosystems that provide water filtration, flood control, and habitat for numerous species. Ramsar's approach emphasises sustainable development, ensuring that wetland benefits are maintained for future generations.

Similarly, the Convention on International Trade in Endangered Species of Wild Fauna and Flora (CITES), in effect since 1975, regulates the trade of over 30,000 species to prevent their exploitation. By categorising species into different appendices based on the level of threat and regulating their trade accordingly, CITES helps maintain viable populations in their natural habitats while allowing for sustainable use.

Global efforts to combat biodiversity loss also involve significant contributions from individual countries. The United States, for instance, has made notable commitments towards biodiversity conservation. Through initiatives like the America the Beautiful Challenge, the U.S. aims to conserve at least 30 percent of its lands and waters by 2030. This public-private partnership funds ecosystem restoration projects that enhance watershed resilience, connectivity, and equitable access to nature. Additionally, agencies like USAID invest extensively in international biodiversity conservation, supporting wildlife protection, ecosystem resilience, and community-based conservation efforts worldwide. In 2021 alone, USAID allocated $319.5 million towards various biodiversity conservation activities (OFFICE OF THE SPOKESPERSON, 2022).

Furthermore, inclusive conservation efforts are critical. Indigenous peoples and local communities play a significant role in managing and conserving biodiversity. Indigenous territories often overlap with many of the world's protected areas and intact ecosystems. Recognising their stewardship, programmes like the Forest Tenure Pledge aim to support Indigenous Peoples' rights and capacities to manage their lands sustainably. Partnerships with organisations such as the Forest Stewardship Council amplify Indigenous voices and facilitate their participation in global conservation efforts (OFFICE OF THE SPOKESPERSON, 2022).

To enhance these collaborative efforts, promoting a one-health approach is gaining traction. This holistic strategy recognises the interconnectedness of human, animal, and environmental health. By addressing issues at this nexus, such as zoonotic diseases and climate-sensitive illnesses, One Health initiatives contribute to healthier ecosystems and communities. Global collaborations under the Mekong-US Partnership and support for platforms like the South America Network for One Health exemplify such integrative approaches (OFFICE OF THE SPOKESPERSON, 2022).

Bringing It All Together

In this chapter, the multifaceted approach to biodiversity projects has been thoroughly explored. Various levels of implementation, from local communities to global collaborations, illustrate the comprehensive efforts undertaken to preserve and enhance biodiversity. By focussing on habitat preservation, sustainable resource use, climate change mitigation, and improving habitat connectivity, these projects aim to build resilient ecosystems capable of withstanding environmental challenges. The involvement of governments, NGOs, corporations, and academic institutions highlights a collective commitment to addressing biodiversity loss through innovative and coordinated actions.

Stakeholder participation at different scales underscores the importance of collaboration in achieving sustainable biodiversity outcomes. Local-level initiatives involve community engagement and leveraging traditional knowledge; national efforts emphasise policy frameworks and large-scale habitat corridors; and global collaborations foster international treaties and research partnerships. These varied approaches combine to create a robust strategy for biodiversity conservation, ensuring that both immediate and long-term ecological health are prioritised. Through these concerted efforts, the chapter demonstrates how integrated actions are essential for maintaining the delicate balance of our planet's natural systems.

Reference List

C40 Knowledge Community . (2024). C40knowledgehub.org. https://www.c40knowledgehub.org/s/article/How-to-enhance-restore-and-protect-biodiversity-in-your-city

Habitat Connectivity: A Win for Biodiversity . (n.d.). National Caucus of Environmental Legislators. https://www.ncelenviro.org/articles/habitat-connectivity-a-win-for-biodiversity/

Ibrahim, I., & Abdul Aziz, N. (2012). *The roles of international NGOs in the conservation of the biodiversity of wetlands* . *Procedia: Social and Behavioural Sciences* , *42* , 242-247. https://doi.org/10.1016/j.sbspro.2012.04.187

Newell, R., Dale, A., & Lister, N.-M. (2022). *An integrated climate-biodiversity framework to improve planning and policy: an application to wildlife crossings and landscape connectivity* . Ecology and Society. https://doi.org/10.5751/es-12999-270123

OFFICE OF THE SPOKESPERSON. (2022, December 15). *Highlighting U.S. Efforts to Combat the Biodiversity Crisis, United States Department of State* . United States Department of State. https://www.state.gov/highlighting-u-s-efforts-to-combat-the-biodiversity-crisis/

Padilla, Zinke, and Beyer Announce Bipartisan Bill to Strengthen Habitat Connectivity and Migration Corridors—Senator Alex Padilla . (2024, June 24). Senator Alex Padilla. https://www.padilla.senate.gov/newsroom/press-releases/padilla-zinke-beyer-announce-bipartisan-bill-to-strengthen-habitat-connectivity-and-migration-corridors/

Dr. Anthonysamy David

Saghira. (2024). *NGOs in conservation and biodiversity protection: Role, challenges, and impact* . NGO Feed. https://ngofeed.com/ngos-in-conservation-and-biodiversity-protection/

Unit B. (2017, December 4). *Biodiversity-related Conventions* . Www.cbd.int. https://www.cbd.int/brc

Weiskopf, S. R. (2020, September 1). *Climate change has effects on biodiversity, ecosystems, ecosystem services, and natural resource management in the United States* . Science of the Total Environment. https://doi.org/10.1016/j.scitotenv.2020.137782

admin. (2021, November 29). *Community engagement for the restoration of local ecosystems*

—Rewilding Academy . Rewilding Academy: https://rewilding.academy/ecosystem-restoration/community-engagement-for-the-restoration-of-local-ecosystems/

Chapter 5

Biodiversity in India

B iodiversity in India is a testament to the country's rich and varied ecosystems, which range from dense forests and wetlands to arid deserts and extensive marine environments. This remarkable diversity is not just limited to the types of landscapes but extends to the species that inhabit them. India's unique climatic conditions and geographical features contribute to the existence of numerous ecosystems, each supporting vast species diversity. These habitats include tropical rainforests, temperate forests, grasslands, savannas, coastal regions, and even high-altitude areas in the Himalayas, creating an intricate web of life forms.

This chapter delves into the multifaceted aspects of India's biodiversity. It will explore the diverse ecosystems and the specific flora and fauna they support. The chapter also focuses on the conservation efforts undertaken to preserve these natural riches, integrating traditional knowledge with modern science. Additionally, it will discuss the cultural and economic value of biodiversity in India and emphasize the importance of public awareness in conservation initiatives. By understanding these elements, readers can appreciate the critical role India plays in global biodiversity conservation.

Rich Biodiversity

India's status as a megadiverse country plays a crucial role in our understanding of global biodiversity. Recognized as one of the world's 17 megadiverse countries, India accounts for approximately 7-8% of all recorded species while covering only 2.4% of the world's land area. This exceptional richness in biodiversity places India among an elite group of nations that together harbor more than 70% of Earth's biodiversity.

A key aspect of India's biodiversity is its numerous ecosystems, each supporting vast species diversity. From dense forests and vibrant wetlands to arid deserts and extensive marine environments, these diverse ecosystems serve as habitats for a multitude of plant and animal species. These varied habitats result from India's wide range of climatic conditions and physical features that include mountain ranges, river systems, and coastlines. For instance, the Himalayan region, with its cold climate and high altitudes, contrasts starkly with the hot, dry Thar Desert, each hosting unique flora and fauna adapted to their specific environments (India, n.d.).

India's biodiversity is further characterized by a significant number of endemic species—plants and animals found nowhere else in the world. Endemism in India is notably high across various taxa. Studies have documented that about 12.6% of mammals, 4.5% of birds, 45.8% of reptiles, 55.8% of amphibians, and 33% of plants are endemic to the country (Biodiversity in India, n.d.). This high level of endemism underscores India's irreplaceable role in global biodiversity conservation efforts. Protecting these species is vital as their loss would represent a permanent diminishment of world biodiversity.

One of the most striking features of India's biodiversity is its range of ecosystems. The nation's landscape includes forests that vary from tropical rainforests in the Western Ghats to temperate forests in the Himalayas. Each type of forest ecosystem harbors distinct species assemblages and contributes differently to ecological processes such as carbon sequestration and climate regulation.

Wetland ecosystems in India, including mangroves, freshwater lakes, and marshes, support a wide array of species and provide critical services such as flood control, water purification, and fisheries resources. Coastal and marine ecosystems, particularly along the western and eastern coastlines, sustain rich biodiversity, including coral reefs, seagrass beds, and marine fauna such as dolphins, whales, and a myriad of fish species (India, n.d.). Deserts, like the Thar Desert, offer a different set of challenges and opportunities for life;

organisms here exhibit remarkable adaptations to extreme temperatures and scarce water availability.

Grasslands and savannas, often overlooked in discussions of biodiversity, play a significant role in supporting large herbivores and predators and are essential for maintaining ecological balance. The fragmented yet biodiverse ecosystems of India contribute to the intricate web of life and highlight the importance of habitat connectivity for wildlife movement and genetic exchange.

The Indian subcontinent, due to its historical and geographic isolation, has been a cradle for evolution, leading to the development of unique species over millions of years. This evolutionary history is reflected in the diversity of life forms present today, marking India as a pivotal region for both conservation biology and evolutionary studies. Efforts to catalog and understand this biodiversity are ongoing, with estimates suggesting that hundreds of thousands of species remain to be described.

Conservation efforts in India are strengthening the protection of these ecosystems. National parks, wildlife sanctuaries, and biosphere reserves cover significant portions of the country's landscapes and are crucial for preserving biodiversity. While these protected areas provide safe havens for many species, they also face challenges such as habitat encroachment, climate change, and human-wildlife conflict.

Public awareness and involvement are key components in the conservation of India's biodiversity. Programs aimed at educating the public about the importance of biodiversity, such as community-led conservation projects and eco-tourism initiatives, help bridge the gap between local communities and conservation goals. Increasing public understanding of biodiversity's value can foster greater support for conservation measures and sustainable practices.

India's commitment to biodiversity is also reflected in its participation in international agreements and collaborations. As a member of IUCN since 1969, India has worked alongside other nations to address global biodiversity issues. The integration of traditional knowledge with modern conservation strategies presents an opportunity to harness the strengths of both approaches, ensuring more effective management of natural resources.

Documenting and sharing biodiversity information through platforms like the India Biodiversity Portal facilitates data-driven decision-making and promotes transparency in conservation efforts. Open access to biodiversity data allows researchers, policymakers, and conservationists to collaborate and devise well-informed strategies to safeguard India's natural heritage.

Diverse Ecosystems

India, a land of astonishing diversity, boasts a range of ecosystems that contribute to its rich tapestry of biodiversity. From the towering peaks of the Himalayas to the arid expanses of the Thar Desert, each ecosystem supports unique species adapted to their specific environments. Exploring these varied ecosystems reveals the intricate balance of flora and fauna that make India one of the world's biological treasure troves.

The Himalayas, stretching along the northern borders of India, are home to some of the most unique flora and fauna on the planet. This vast mountain range includes diverse ecosystems from dense forested areas to alpine meadows and barren rocky terrains at high altitudes. Species in this region have evolved to withstand the extreme conditions and altitude variations. The elusive snow leopard roams the higher elevations, perfectly camouflaged against the snowy backdrop. The Himalayan monal, Nepal's national bird, exhibits iridescent plumage and thrives in the cooler climates. Additionally, the region is famed for its rhododendron forests, which burst into a riot of colors during the flowering season. These forests are not just visually striking but also crucial habitats for various bird and insect species.

Moving southward, the Western Ghats, also known as the Sahyadri Mountains, present a stark contrast to the chilly heights of the Himalayas. Recognized as one of the world's eight "hottest" biodiversity hotspots, the Western Ghats are characterized by moist tropical forests that receive heavy rainfall. These lush forests are rich in endemic species—organisms found nowhere else on Earth. The lion-tailed macaque, an endangered primate, swings through the canopies of these forests, while the ground below hosts numerous amphibian species like the Malabar gliding frog. Birdlife is abundant, with species such as the Great Hornbill and the Nilgiri flycatcher making their homes in these verdant landscapes. The plant life is equally impressive, with thousands of species including vibrant orchids and ancient trees that form dense, impenetrable thickets.

In stark contrast to the humid Western Ghats lies the Thar Desert in the northwest of India. This arid region, also known as the Great Indian Desert, presents an environment where only the toughest organisms survive. Xerophytic vegetation, such as cacti and thorny shrubs, dominate the landscape, adapted to the harsh climatic conditions with minimal water requirements. The Khejri tree, vital for the local ecosystem, provides fodder during drought periods and helps in soil stabilization. The wildlife here is diverse and includes species uniquely adapted to the desert environment. The Indian bustard, a critically endangered bird, and the Indian gazelle, or chinkara, demonstrate remarkable adaptations to cope with the scarcity of water. In addition to their ecological roles, these species add to the cultural heritage of the region, often finding mention in local folklore and traditions.

Further east, the Sundarbans offer a completely different ecological experience. This region houses the world's largest mangrove forest and is an exceptional example of a coastal ecosystem. The Sundarbans span across the delta of the Padma, Meghna, and Brahmaputra rivers, creating a labyrinth of waterways and small islands covered in thick mangrove forests. These waters support a myriad of species, with the Royal Bengal Tiger being the most iconic inhabitant. The tiger population here is adapted to a semi-aquatic lifestyle, swimming between islands and hunting in the brackish waters. Mangrove trees themselves play a critical ecological role; their complex root systems trap sediment and reduce coastal erosion while providing habitat for fish, crabs, and other marine life. Various species of migratory birds, estuarine crocodiles, and the Ganges River Dolphin are also found within the Sundarbans, showcasing a unique balance of terrestrial and aquatic life forms.

These diverse ecosystems illustrate India's unparalleled biodiversity and underscore its significance in global conservation efforts. Each ecosystem, from the high-altitude Himalayan meadows to the arid expanse of the Thar Desert, contributes uniquely to the country's natural heritage. The Himalayas, with their range of altitudinal zones, enable the existence of highly specialized species. The Western Ghats' moist tropical forests sustain a wealth of endemic organisms that are vital to maintaining ecological balance. The Thar Desert exemplifies resilience and adaptability under extreme conditions, while the Sundarbans showcase the harmony between land and water-based life forms.

Understanding and preserving these ecosystems is not merely an environmental imperative but also a recognition of the natural beauty and cultural significance they hold. Conservation strategies must emphasize protecting these unique habitats from threats such as deforestation, climate change, and human encroachment. Sustainable practices and community-led initiatives can play a pivotal role in ensuring that future generations continue to benefit from and marvel at India's rich biodiversity.

Species Diversity

India's remarkable biodiversity is a testament to its range of ecosystems, from the towering Himalayas to the coastal mangroves. This subpoint will highlight India's species variety, focusing on its iconic animals, lesser-known flora and fauna, the crucial roles these species play in maintaining ecosystem health, and the high levels of endemic species found nowhere else in the world.

Home to Iconic Animals

India is globally renowned for being home to some of the most iconic and majestic animals. The Bengal tiger, with its striking orange coat and black stripes, is not only a symbol of strength and power but also a critical apex predator that maintains balance within its habitat. Found predominantly in national parks like Sundarbans and Ranthambore, Bengal tigers are integral to the health of their ecosystems.

Similarly, the Indian elephant plays a vital role in shaping forest environments. As a keystone species, elephants influence the structure of vegetation through their feeding habits, helping maintain the ecological integrity of forests. They are commonly seen in reserves such as Kaziranga National Park and Corbett National Park.

Rich Variety of Lesser-Known Species

Beyond the well-known wildlife, India harbors a myriad of lesser-known plants, insects, and microorganisms. These species, although not as famous, are incredibly important for the functioning of ecosystems. India's flora includes an array of medicinal plants like the neem tree, known for its various health benefits. Insects such as bees and butterflies are essential pollinators, ensuring the reproduction of many flowering plants.

Microorganisms in the soil play critical roles in nutrient cycling, decomposing organic matter and enhancing soil fertility. For instance, mycorrhizal fungi form symbiotic relationships with plant roots, facilitating water and nutrient uptake. The rich array of lesser-known species often goes unnoticed, yet they are indispensable to ecosystem health and resilience.

Crucial Roles in Maintaining Ecosystem Health

Each species within an ecosystem contributes to its overall health and functionality. Predators control prey populations, preventing any single species from becoming too dominant and thus maintaining balance. Herbivores like deer and antelopes help in seed dispersal and vegetation management.

Plants and trees contribute to carbon sequestration, reducing the impact of climate change by absorbing carbon dioxide from the atmosphere. Water bodies within forests are kept clean by various aquatic organisms that filter pollutants. Insect pollinators support food production by fertilizing crops, which is crucial for human survival.

For example, the Western Ghats, one of the most biodiverse regions in the world, is home to numerous endemic species of plants and animals. This mountain range supports unique flora such as the Neelakurinji flower, which blooms once every twelve years. The presence of such diverse and unique species ensures the stability and productivity of ecosystems.

It is well established that disruptions in these delicate balances can lead to ecosystem collapse, affecting both biodiversity and human populations dependent on these ecosystems. The extinction of a single species can have a cascading effect, leading to unforeseen consequences for the entire ecosystem.

High Levels of Endemism

India boasts high levels of endemism, with many species found nowhere else in the world. The Western Ghats alone host over 1,500 endemic plant species. Likewise, the Andaman and Nicobar Islands harbor unique species such as the Nicobar pigeon and the Dugong, a sea cow.

The significance of endemism lies in its reflection of a region's evolutionary history and uniqueness. Endemic species are often adapted to specific environmental conditions and contribute to the genetic diversity of their ecosystems. Their conservation is crucial, as the loss of endemic species would mean a permanent loss of biodiversity unique to India.

To illustrate, the Asiatic lion, restricted to the Gir Forest National Park, symbolizes successful conservation efforts to protect this unique species from extinction. Similarly, the Lion-tailed macaque, endemic to the Western Ghats, represents the rich primate diversity of India.

Conservation Efforts and Challenges

Despite its rich biodiversity, India faces significant challenges in conserving its natural heritage. Habitat destruction, pollution, and overexploitation of resources pose severe threats. However, numerous initiatives by the government, non-governmental organizations (NGOs), and local communities aim to address these issues.

Programs like Project Tiger and Project Elephant have been instrumental in protecting these flagship species and their habitats. Additionally, community-led conservation efforts, such as those by indigenous tribes, integrate traditional ecological knowledge with modern practices, enhancing the effectiveness of conservation strategies.

International collaborations and adherence to global agreements further bolster India's conservation efforts. Sustainable resource management, habitat restoration, and targeted conservation of endangered species are part of a multifaceted approach to preserving biodiversity.

Public awareness campaigns and education programs play a crucial role in fostering a sense of responsibility among the populace. Understanding the importance of biodiversity motivates people to support and participate in conservation initiatives.

Conservation Efforts

India is home to a rich mosaic of ecosystems, which host an incredible diversity of flora and fauna. To safeguard its invaluable biodiversity, the country has launched various conservation initiatives, integrating governmental action with community involvement. This chapter delves into India's efforts to preserve its natural heritage through the establishment of protected areas, successful projects like Project Tiger and Project Elephant, and the integration of community-led conservation efforts. We will also discuss the ongoing challenges that necessitate more coordinated approaches.

India's pioneering efforts in biodiversity conservation are evident through the creation of national parks, wildlife sanctuaries, and biosphere reserves. These protected areas serve as refuges for endangered species and vital habitats, ensuring the survival of diverse ecological communities. National parks such as Jim Corbett, Kaziranga, and Bandipur play a crucial role in conserving both flora and fauna, providing safe havens where human activities are restricted.

The establishment of wildlife sanctuaries further augments conservation efforts by protecting specific species and their habitats. Sanctuaries like Periyar and Bharatpur offer controlled environments that mitigate human-wildlife conflict while promoting breeding and rehabilitation programs. Biosphere reserves, on the other hand, integrate conservation with sustainable resource use, aiming to balance the needs of local communities with environmental preservation. The Nilgiri Biosphere Reserve is a prime example, showcasing how these areas can foster both biodiversity and socio-economic growth.

Among the many conservation projects in India, two stand out for their remarkable success: Project Tiger and Project Elephant. Launched in 1973, Project Tiger was a response to the alarming decline in the tiger population. The project focuses on habitat preservation, anti-poaching measures, and mitigating human-tiger conflicts. By creating dedicated tiger reserves and implementing stringent protection protocols, Project Tiger has bolstered the Bengal tiger population and safeguarded essential tiger habitats. As a result, parks like Ranthambore and Sundarbans have become thriving centers for tiger conservation (TinkerChild, 2023).

Similarly, Project Elephant, initiated in 1992, addresses the critical need to protect elephant habitats and mitigate human-elephant conflicts. The project aims to manage and improve existing elephant corridors, prevent poaching, and educate locals about coexisting peacefully with elephants. Over the years, initiatives under Project Elephant have led to the establishment of several elephant reserves and the implementation of measures to reduce agricultural damage caused by roaming herds. The success of these flagship projects underscores the importance of focused conservation strategies and the positive impact they can have on individual species and broader ecosystems.

Community-led conservation efforts are another pillar of India's biodiversity preservation strategy, recognizing that local communities possess valuable traditional knowledge and a vested interest in maintaining their surrounding environment. Initiatives such as the Joint Forest Management program encourage local participation in forest conservation, enabling communities to manage resources sustainably and share in the benefits derived from them. This inclusive approach empowers people at the grassroots level, fostering a sense of stewardship and responsibility towards nature.

Examples of successful community-led efforts include the Chipko Movement in the 1970s, where villagers in Uttarakhand protected trees from being felled by hugging them, thus raising awareness about the importance of forest conservation. Similarly, the Vikalp Sangam initiative brings together diverse groups to devise community-based solutions for ecosystem management, highlighting the power of collective action in safeguarding biodiversity. By integrating traditional ecological knowledge with modern conservation practices, these efforts contribute significantly to the resilience and sustainability of India's natural landscapes.

Despite the considerable successes, India's biodiversity conservation endeavors face ongoing challenges that demand more coordinated and comprehensive approaches. Habitat loss remains one of the most pressing threats, driven by rapid urbanization, agricultural expansion, and infrastructure development. Deforestation not only fragments animal habitats but also disrupts biological corridors essential for species migration and genetic exchange. Addressing habitat loss requires stricter enforcement of land-use regulations and innovative solutions that align development goals with environmental priorities.

Furthermore, poaching and illegal wildlife trade pose severe threats to several iconic species. Despite stringent laws, the demand for animal parts in traditional medicine and the black market continues to fuel poaching activities. Enhanced funding, better surveillance technology, and community vigilance are essential to curbing illegal hunting and trafficking. Projects like Wildlife Trust of India's anti-poaching units illustrate how collaborative efforts between government bodies and NGOs can effectively tackle this menace.

Human-wildlife conflict is another significant challenge, exacerbated by encroachment into wildlife habitats and the shrinking availability of natural resources. Crop destruction, livestock predation, and occasional human fatalities lead to retaliatory killings of wildlife, undermining conservation efforts. Innovative mitigation strategies, such as the construction of wildlife corridors, compensation schemes for affected farmers, and community awareness programs, are vital to reducing these conflicts and fostering harmonious coexistence.

Climate change adds yet another layer of complexity to biodiversity conservation. Rising temperatures, altered weather patterns, and shifting ecosystems impact species' survival and behavior, leading to changes in migration routes and breeding cycles. Adaptation measures, including habitat restoration and the establishment of climate-resilient conservation zones, are crucial to ensuring that species can thrive despite climatic fluctuations. Research and monitoring initiatives, like those undertaken by the Nature Conservation Foundation, provide valuable insights into how climate change affects high-altitude wildlife and inform adaptive conservation strategies.

Traditional Knowledge and Economic Value

India's rich biodiversity is deeply intertwined with its indigenous communities, whose traditional knowledge has been instrumental in managing natural resources sustainably for centuries. These communities possess a profound understanding of their local ecosystems, gained through generations of close interaction with nature. This traditional ecological knowledge (TEK) offers valuable insights into the functioning of various species and habitats, which can greatly enhance modern conservation practices.

Indigenous communities have long practiced resource management methodologies that emphasize balance and sustainability. For example, shifting cultivation, also known as slash-and-burn agriculture, has been used by many indigenous groups without leading to depletion of forest resources. This practice allows agricultural fields to regenerate, maintaining soil fertility and supporting biodiversity. Moreover, the rotational use of these areas minimizes the risk of overharvesting and promotes habitat diversity.

Traditional ecological knowledge can complement contemporary conservation efforts in numerous ways. One significant benefit is the ability of TEK to provide baseline data on species and ecosystem conditions over extended periods. As noted by Jessen et al. (2021), indigenous observations have been critical for monitoring species and ecosystems, enabling the detection of ecological changes that might go unnoticed with short-term scientific studies. By integrating this knowledge with scientific methods, conservationists can develop more effective strategies to manage and restore biodiversity.

Biodiversity underpins several key industries in India, including agriculture, medicine, and tourism. In agriculture, biodiversity plays a crucial role in crop diversity, pest control, and soil health. Diverse plant species ensure food security by offering a range of crops resistant to different pests and diseases. Additionally, the presence of various pollinators, such as bees and butterflies, is essential for the pollination of many crops, directly impacting agricultural productivity.

In the realm of medicine, India's biodiversity contributes significantly through the provision of medicinal plants and other natural resources used in traditional healing practices. Numerous pharmaceutical compounds have been derived from plants native to Indian ecosystems, showcasing the vital link between biodiversity and healthcare. For instance, the neem tree (Azadirachta indica), commonly found in India, has been used for centuries for its medicinal properties and continues to be an important source of natural remedies.

Tourism is another sector heavily reliant on biodiversity. Ecotourism, which focuses on sustainable travel to natural areas, allows tourists to experience the country's unique wildlife and landscapes. National parks, wildlife sanctuaries, and biosphere reserves attract visitors from around the world, generating significant revenue for local economies. This influx of funds can support conservation efforts, creating a positive feedback loop where tourism helps finance the protection of biodiversity.

Beyond these direct economic benefits, biodiversity provides essential ecosystem services that support human well-being and economic activities. Pollination, water purification, and climate regulation are just a few examples of these services. Pollinators play a vital role in the reproductive processes of many plants, ensuring the production of fruits, vegetables, and seeds. Without these organisms, agricultural yields would drop, leading to food shortages and increased economic strain.

Water purification is another critical service provided by healthy ecosystems. Wetlands, forests, and grasslands act as natural filters, removing pollutants from water bodies and maintaining water quality. These natural systems are far more cost-effective than man-made water treatment facilities and offer additional benefits such as habitat preservation and carbon sequestration.

Climate regulation is perhaps one of the most significant ecosystem services offered by biodiversity. Forests, oceans, and other ecosystems act as carbon sinks, absorbing and storing carbon dioxide from the atmosphere. This process helps mitigate the impacts of climate change by reducing greenhouse gas concentrations. Additionally, diverse ecosystems are more resilient to climatic shifts, maintaining their functionality and continuing to provide essential services even under stress.

Given these multifaceted benefits of biodiversity, it is imperative to integrate traditional ecological knowledge into modern conservation frameworks. Collaborative efforts that recognize the value of both indigenous knowledge and scientific research will be more effective in addressing the complex challenges of biodiversity loss. Such partnerships should also be restitutive and rights-based, ensuring that indigenous communities retain control over their knowledge and receive equitable benefits from its application (Ogar et al., 2020).

Public awareness and education about biodiversity are equally crucial in fostering a sense of stewardship among all societal sectors. Educational programs that highlight the cultural and economic importance of biodiversity can encourage more people to engage in conservation activities. By raising awareness about the interconnectedness of ecosystems and human well-being, these programs can promote behaviours and policies that support sustainable development.

Final Insights

The chapter has delved into the rich biodiversity of India, highlighting its varied ecosystems from the Himalayas to the Thar Desert. It has underscored the significance of India's endemic species and the efforts undertaken to catalogue and conserve this diverse life. Various conservation strategies, including national parks and community-led initiatives, were discussed to emphasize the importance of safeguarding these habitats. The text also examined how traditional knowledge integrates with modern conservation practices, offering a holistic approach to preserving biodiversity.

Public awareness plays a crucial role in these conservation efforts, bridging the gap between local communities and ecological goals. Educational programs and eco-tourism initiatives have been effective in fostering an understanding of biodiversity's cultural and economic values. By raising awareness about the importance of conserving biodiversity, India can ensure that its

Dr. Anthonysamy David

natural heritage is preserved for future generations. This comprehensive approach not only protects ecosystems but also enhances the quality of life by maintaining the natural balance critical for human survival.

Reference List

Biodiversity in India . (n.d.). India Biodiversity Portal. https://indiabiodiversity.org/page/show/4246006

CK-12 Foundation. (2024). *Identify the hotspots in India known for biodiversity* . Retrieved from https://www.ck12.org/flexi/life-science/importance-of-biodiversity/identify-the-hotspots-in-india-known-for-biodiversity./

Chaudhari, H. (2022, December 21). *Biodiversity in India - Heemali Chaudhari - Medium* . Medium; Medium. https:// theheemalichaudhari.medium.com/biodiversity-in-india-b9eee5a72c8d

From Tigers to Trees: Navigating Through The Scenario Of Loss Of Biodiversity In India . (2023). The United Indian. https://theunitedindian.com/ news/blog?loss-of-biodiversity-in-India&b=136&c=1

India . (n.d.). IUCN. https://www.iucn.org/our-work/region/asia/countries/india

Jessen, T. D., Ban, N. C., Claxton, N. X., & Darimont, C. T. (2021, November 15). *Contributions of Indigenous Knowledge to ecological and evolutionary understanding* .

Frontiers in Ecology and the Environment. https://doi.org/10.1002/fee.2435

Karanth, K. K., Kramer, R. A., Qian, S. S., & Christensen, N. L. (2008, September 1). *Examining conservation attitudes, perspectives, and challenges in India* . Biological Conservation. https://doi.org/10.1016/j.biocon.2008.06.027

Ogar, E., Pecl, G., & Mustonen, T. (2020, August). *Science Must Embrace Traditional and Indigenous Knowledge to Solve Our Biodiversity Crisis* . One Earth. https://doi.org/10.1016/j.oneear.2020.07.006

School Dekho. (n.d.). *Exploring India's rich biodiversity: A journey through its ecosystems* . Retrieved October 18, 2023, from https://www.schooldekho.org/school/blog/details/

Exploring-India's-Rich-Biodiversity:-A-Journey-Through-Its-Ecosystems-1254

TinkerChild. (2023, December 25). *Wildlife Conservation Initiatives in India: A Comprehensive Overview* . TinkerChild; TinkerChild. https://www.tinkerchild.com/post/wildlife-conservation-initiatives-in-india-balancing-nature-s-harmony

Chapter 6

Biodiversity Conservation in India: Strategies and Perspectives

Biodiversity conservation in India is pivotal for maintaining the ecological balance and health of its diverse ecosystems. The country's commitment to preserving its flora and fauna is reflected in a robust legal framework, which includes critical legislative measures like the Wildlife Protection Act, Forest Conservation Act, and National Biodiversity Act. These laws not only aim to protect endangered species and habitats but also seek to integrate biodiversity considerations into broader policy domains. India's rich natural heritage faces numerous challenges, such as habitat loss, climate change, and pollution, necessitating a comprehensive approach to conservation that balances development needs with environmental preservation.

This chapter delves into the various strategies and perspectives on biodiversity conservation in India. It examines the effectiveness and gaps in existing policies, emphasising the need for further integration of biodiversity goals into sectors like agriculture, urban planning, and industrial development. Additionally, the chapter highlights successful initiatives and offers recommendations for enhancing conservation efforts. By exploring the intersections between policy frameworks, community involvement, sustainable practices, and ecosystem services, this chapter aims to provide a holistic understanding of the steps required to conserve India's biodiversity while supporting sustainable development.

Dr. Anthonysamy David

Policy Frameworks

A strong legal system that aims to safeguard India's diverse flora and fauna serves as the foundation for its commitment to biodiversity conservation. This section examines key legislative measures such as the Wildlife Protection Act, Forest Conservation Act, and the National Biodiversity Act, highlighting their successes and identifying areas where further integration into broader policies is needed. Additionally, it emphasises revising industrial development strategies to harmonise with biodiversity conservation goals.

The Wildlife Protection Act of 1972 stands as a cornerstone law for biodiversity conservation in India. Its primary focus is on the protection of wild animals, birds, and plants. The act categorises species under different schedules based on their conservation status, providing varying levels of protection. For instance, Schedule I lists highly endangered species such as the Bengal tiger and the Indian rhinoceros, ensuring stringent penalties for offences related to these animals. One notable success of this legislation is Project Tiger, launched in 1973, which has significantly increased the population of tigers in India. Similarly, conservation efforts for species like the Asiatic lion and one-horned rhinoceros have shown positive trends under this act.

Complementing the Wildlife Protection Act is the Forest Conservation Act of 1980, which regulates the diversion of forest land for non-forest purposes. This act mandates that any project involving the use of forest land must receive approval from the central government, ensuring that ecological assessments are conducted before proceeding. A significant outcome of this legislation is the reduction in deforestation rates and the preservation of critical habitats. For example, the act has played a crucial role in protecting unique ecosystems like the mangroves of the Sundarbans and the coral reefs of the Andaman Islands.

Another pivotal piece of legislation is the National Biodiversity Act of 2002. This act was enacted to fulfil India's obligations under the Convention on Biological Diversity (CBD) and focusses on the conservation of biological resources, sustainable use of their components, and fair and equitable sharing of benefits arising out of the use of biological resources. It established the National Biodiversity Authority (NBA), State Biodiversity Boards (SBBs), and Biodiversity Management Committees (BMCs) at the local level. These bodies work collaboratively to ensure the protection of biodiversity, regulate access to biological resources, and promote sustainable practices. Successes under this act include the documentation of traditional knowledge associated with biological resources and the formulation of People's Biodiversity Registers.

While the existing legal frameworks have yielded significant achievements, there is an urgent need to integrate biodiversity concerns into broader policy domains such as agriculture, urban planning, and industrial development. Agricultural practices often lead to habitat destruction, pesticide pollution, and a decline in species diversity. Integrating biodiversity-friendly practices like agroforestry and organic farming can help mitigate these impacts. Urban planning should also prioritise green spaces, create urban wildlife corridors, and implement policies that reduce light and noise pollution, benefiting both biodiversity and human populations.

In addition to integrating biodiversity into agricultural and urban planning policies, it is essential to revise industrial development strategies. Industries often exert tremendous pressure on natural habitats through land conversion, resource extraction, and pollution. Aligning industrial activities with biodiversity conservation involves adopting cleaner technologies, implementing stringent environmental impact assessments, and promoting corporate social responsibility initiatives focused on conservation.

To foster better integration of biodiversity concerns into these broader policies, a guideline would be beneficial for policymakers and stakeholders. Here are some recommended actions:

1. **Cross-Sectoral Policies** : Develop cross-sectoral policies that explicitly incorporate biodiversity conservation objectives in

agriculture, urban development, and industrial strategies.

2. **Environmental Impact Assessments (EIAs)** : Strengthen EIA processes to evaluate and mitigate potential adverse effects on biodiversity before approving projects.

3. **Incentives for Sustainable Practices** : Provide financial incentives and subsidies for adopting biodiversity-friendly practices in agriculture and industry.

4. **Public Awareness and Education** : Promote awareness and education campaigns to highlight the importance of biodiversity and engage communities in conservation efforts.

5. **Enhanced Monitoring and Enforcement** : Improve monitoring systems and enforce existing laws more rigorously to deter violations and ensure compliance.

Implementing these guidelines can help bridge the gap between biodiversity conservation and other developmental sectors, creating a cohesive approach towards sustainable development.

Despite strong legislative frameworks, challenges like human-wildlife conflict, habitat fragmentation, and enforcement difficulties persist. Human-wildlife conflict arises due to expanding human populations and shrinking natural habitats, leading to frequent encounters between humans and wildlife. Such conflicts often result in loss of life and property, underscoring the need for effective mitigation strategies like community-based conflict resolution mechanisms and compensation schemes for affected individuals.

Roads and dams, for example, disrupt wildlife corridors, which impedes animal migration and genetic flow. To address this, it is crucial to design infrastructure projects that consider ecological connectivity, such as building wildlife overpasses and underpasses.

Enforcement remains a significant challenge despite comprehensive laws. Limited resources, corruption, and infrastructural constraints hinder effective implementation. Strengthening enforcement agencies, increasing funding, and leveraging technology—such as remote sensing and drone surveillance—can enhance monitoring and compliance.

Community Involvement

Local communities play a crucial role in successful biodiversity conservation. They possess an intimate understanding of their local ecosystems, which is essential for effective conservation strategies. Historically, various indigenous and rural communities have lived in harmony with their natural surroundings, relying on their resources for sustenance while ensuring that these resources are not overexploited. The involvement of local communities in conservation efforts can lead to more sustainable outcomes, as these communities often have a vested interest in preserving the environment that supports their livelihoods.

Initiatives like Joint Forest Management (JFM) have been instrumental in empowering communities to manage and protect forests. JFM involves collaboration between village communities and government forest departments to share responsibilities and benefits from forest resources. This initiative promotes community participation in forest management activities such as afforestation, soil and moisture conservation, and forest protection against illegal activities. For example, JFM has led to the regeneration of degraded forests and improved the socio-economic conditions of participating communities by providing them with alternative livelihood options. By integrating local knowledge and enhancing the capacity of communities, JFM contributes to more effective and inclusive forest management practices (DeepBlueInk, 2024).

Community Conserved Areas (CCAs) further demonstrate the positive impact of community involvement on conservation outcomes. CCAs are regions where local communities manage and protect biodiversity through traditional or contemporary practices. These areas are often rich in cultural and biological diversity due to the long-standing stewardship of the communities. CCAs showcase that when communities have the authority and support to manage their lands, they can achieve significant conservation successes. In India, several CCAs have been recognised for their contribution to conserving endangered species and habitats, showing that empowering communities can lead to robust and lasting conservation achievements (Traditional Knowledge and Conservation of Biodiversity for Sustainable Livelihoods by Tribal Communities in Southern India, 2024).

Integrating traditional knowledge and practices into local conservation efforts is another critical aspect of community-based biodiversity conservation. Traditional Ecological Knowledge (TEK) encompasses the wisdom, practices, and beliefs developed by indigenous and local communities over generations through direct interaction with their environment. TEK includes sustainable land-use practices such as selective logging, controlled burning, and rotational agriculture, which help maintain ecosystem balance and biodiversity. For instance, indigenous fire management practices have been proven to reduce fuel loads, prevent large-scale wildfires, and promote the growth of fire-adapted plant species. By combining TEK with modern scientific approaches, conservation programmes can be more adaptive, resilient, and effective in addressing ecological challenges (DeepBlueInk, 2024).

Joint Forest Management (JFM) guidelines provide a structured approach to involving local communities in forest conservation. These guidelines outline the formation of Joint Forest Management Committees (JFMCs) at the village level, which include representatives from both the community and the forest department. JFMCs are responsible for preparing microplans that detail forest management activities, benefit-sharing mechanisms, and monitoring processes. The guidelines also emphasise capacity-building through training and awareness programmes to equip communities with the necessary skills and knowledge for sustainable forest management. By following these guidelines, JFM ensures that conservation efforts are participatory, transparent, and aligned with the needs and aspirations of local communities (Traditional Knowledge and Conservation of Biodiversity for Sustainable Livelihoods by Tribal Communities in Southern India, 2024).

Community Conserved Areas (CCAs) highlight the importance of community-led conservation initiatives. CCAs are often designated based on traditional governance systems and customary laws that regulate resource use and protect biodiversity. For example, some tribal communities in India have established Sacred Groves, patches of forest preserved for religious and cultural reasons, which serve as important biodiversity hotspots. Recognising and supporting CCAs through legal and policy frameworks can enhance their effectiveness and sustainability. This includes formal recognition of community rights to land and resources, financial support for conservation activities, and capacity-building initiatives to strengthen community governance structures. Integrating CCAs into broader conservation policies can create a network of protected areas that benefit both biodiversity and local communities (DeepBlueInk, 2024).

Involving communities for effective conservation encompasses several strategies that facilitate meaningful engagement and collaboration. Participatory decision-making processes are crucial, as they ensure that community perspectives, values, and priorities are incorporated into conservation planning. Techniques like community-based mapping, joint land-use planning, and consultative forums help build trust and transparency between stakeholders. Capacity-building and training programmes enhance the ability of communities to manage their natural resources sustainably. For example, training in sustainable harvesting techniques, wildlife monitoring, and eco-tourism initiatives can provide alternative livelihoods while promoting conservation goals. Strengthening community institutions and leadership is also vital for sustaining conservation efforts over time (Traditional Knowledge and Conservation of

Biodiversity for Sustainable Livelihoods by Tribal Communities in Southern India, 2024).

Another essential strategy is the exchange of traditional ecological knowledge (TEK) between communities and scientific researchers. Collaborative research projects that integrate TEK with scientific data can offer comprehensive insights into ecosystem dynamics and species behaviour. Participatory monitoring programmes, where community members collect and analyse environmental data, contribute to more effective and locally relevant conservation measures. Additionally, fostering mutual learning and respect between scientists and communities can enhance innovation and adaptive management in conservation practices. By recognising the value of TEK and incorporating it into modern conservation frameworks, we can improve the resilience and sustainability of biodiversity conservation efforts (DeepBlueInk, 2024).

Policy support and legal recognition are fundamental for empowering local communities in biodiversity conservation. Enacting policies that recognise community rights to land, resources, and traditional knowledge can secure their tenure and incentivise sustainable management practices. Legal recognition of customary land tenure systems and community-conserved areas strengthens community governance and safeguards against external threats such as land grabbing, resource exploitation, and industrial development. International instruments like the United Nations Declaration on the Rights of Indigenous Peoples (UNDRIP) and the Convention on Biological Diversity (CBD) provide frameworks for protecting indigenous rights and promoting community-based conservation. National policies should align with these international commitments to ensure that local communities are integral partners in biodiversity conservation efforts (Traditional Knowledge and Conservation of Biodiversity for Sustainable Livelihoods by Tribal Communities in Southern India, 2024).

Providing financial and technical support to community-based conservation initiatives is also crucial. Access to funding, technical assistance, and capacity-building resources enables communities to implement sustainable forestry practices, habitat restoration projects, and alternative livelihood programmes. For instance, grants and partnerships with governments, non-governmental organisations (NGOs), and the private sector can support community forestry projects, eco-tourism ventures, and agroforestry initiatives. These efforts not only contribute to biodiversity conservation but also enhance the socio-economic well-being of local communities. By investing in community-led conservation, we can create a more inclusive and equitable approach to biodiversity preservation (Deep Blue Ink, 2024).

Sustainable Development

Advocating for sustainable land-use practices that benefit both biodiversity and communities is crucial for India's future. Implementing these practices can help maintain ecological stability, improve livelihoods, and ensure the conservation of our rich natural resources.

Agroforestry practices play a significant role in achieving this balance. By integrating trees with crops and livestock on the same land, agroforestry enhances biodiversity, improves soil fertility, and provides multiple outputs like timber, fruits, and fodder. This method creates a diversified farming system that stabilises incomes for local farmers and reduces dependency on single-crop systems, which are more vulnerable to market fluctuations. Agroforestry also helps sequester carbon, contributing to climate change mitigation. For example, the practice of planting nitrogen-fixing trees such as Faidherbia albida in crop fields enriches the soil naturally, decreasing the need for synthetic fertilisers (Keprate et al., 2024).

Organic farming presents another sustainable land-use practice by reducing chemical inputs and promoting healthier ecosystems. Unlike conventional farming, organic farming avoids synthetic pesticides and fertilisers, instead relying on natural processes and cycles. This approach not only protects soil health but also enhances biodiversity by providing habitats for various organisms. Crops grown organically often have better resistance to pests and diseases due to the healthier ecosystem created around them. Additionally, consumers are increasingly favouring organic produce, offering farmers potential economic benefits through premium pricing. For example, organic farms in regions of Maharashtra and Sikkim have shown promising results in boosting local biodiversity and providing sustainable livelihoods for farmers.

Sustainable forestry ensures that forest resources are used in a way that maintains the forest's environmental, social, and economic functions. It involves practices like selective logging, maintaining buffer zones, and replanting trees to prevent deforestation and degradation. Sustainable forestry practices support a renewable resource base while preserving critical habitats for wildlife. These methods also contribute to long-term economic benefits for communities by providing steady supplies of timber and non-timber forest products, ensuring that forest cover is maintained. Additionally, forests managed sustainably can offer eco-tourism opportunities, further diversifying income for local populations.

As India continues to urbanise rapidly, urban biodiversity conservation becomes increasingly essential. Urban areas, though developed, can still play a key role in supporting biodiversity. Incorporating green spaces, such as parks, gardens, and green roofs, into city planning helps maintain ecological balance and provides residents with recreational areas that enhance quality of life. These green spaces serve as mini-ecosystems, supporting various species of birds, insects, and plants. Furthermore, initiatives like urban farming can bring nature closer to city dwellers, creating opportunities for community engagement in sustainability practices. Cities like Gothenburg and Munich have successfully integrated such practices, demonstrating that urban development and biodiversity conservation can coexist effectively (Sustainable Land Management | WILDLABS n.d.).

Supporting Small-Scale Farmers

Supporting small-scale farmers is crucial for encouraging sustainable agricultural practices. One of the main ways to help these farmers is by providing them with access to essential resources. Resources can include things like seeds, tools, and information about farming methods. When farmers have the right tools and information, they can practice sustainable farming techniques more effectively. For example, if a farmer has high-quality seeds that are better suited to their local climate, it can lead to healthier crops and a more productive farm.

Access to credit is another important aspect of supporting small-scale farmers. Many farmers struggle to afford the inputs they need to grow their crops. By providing access to credit, farmers can obtain the money needed to invest in their farms. This might mean buying new equipment or investing in organic fertilisers. When farmers have the financial support they need, they are more likely to adopt sustainable practices. For instance, with a loan, a farmer might be able to purchase a drip irrigation system that conserves water and enhances crop yield.

Technology and Sustainable Practices

Technology plays a vital role in supporting small-scale farmers as well. Innovative farming technologies can help farmers work more efficiently and sustainably. For example, mobile apps can provide farmers with real-time information about weather patterns, market prices, and pest control methods. By having access to this information, farmers can make better decisions about when to plant their crops or how to combat pests without relying on harmful chemicals.

In addition to apps, precision agriculture tools, such as soil sensors, can help farmers monitor the health of their soil. This technology allows farmers to apply fertilisers and water only when needed, reducing waste and environmental impact. The use of such technology can lead to higher yields while also promoting sustainable practices that protect the environment.

Education and Training

Providing education and training is essential for the successful adoption of sustainable agricultural practices. Farmers may not adopt new methods simply because they are unaware of them or do not know how to implement them. Training programmes can teach farmers about different sustainable techniques, such as crop rotation or natural pest management. These programmes can be offered through workshops, online courses, or community training sessions.

For example, a workshop could teach farmers how to create compost from household waste, which can be used to enrich the soil. By showing farmers how to make compost, they can reduce their waste and produce organic fertiliser for their crops. Training can also encourage farmers to share their knowledge with each other, fostering a community of learning and support.

Community Engagement

Community engagement is a key component in supporting small-scale farmers. Involving local communities in decisions about land management is important because it ensures that the strategies implemented reflect their needs and values. When farmers feel that they have a voice in the decision-making process, they are more likely to support and adopt new practices.

For instance, if a community values organic farming, engaging them in the planning process can help tailor practices that align with that value. This might include prioritising the use of natural fertilisers and pest control methods. Community meetings can be held to discuss land use and encourage farmers to share their thoughts and experiences, leading to more sustainable and accepted practices.

Customising Solutions

Every farming community is different, and solutions need to be customised to fit local conditions. Just because a technique works in one area does not mean it will work elsewhere. Local climate, soil type, and community culture all play a role in determining the best practices for sustainable agriculture in a specific area.

For example, a farming community in a hot, dry region may benefit more from drought-resistant crops than one in a cooler, wetter area. Understanding the unique challenges and opportunities that each community faces can lead to better outcomes. Localised support can include helping farmers select appropriate crops or teaching them how to conserve water based on their specific circumstances.

Building Ownership

Fostering a sense of ownership among local communities regarding their farming practices can enhance sustainable methods. When farmers take pride in their techniques and see the benefits firsthand, they are more likely to stick with them. This sense of ownership can be fostered through participation in pilot projects where farmers can try out sustainable practices on a small scale before fully committing.

For example, a project could introduce a few farmers to agroforestry methods, which involve planting trees alongside crops. These farmers could demonstrate the benefits to their peers, showing them how trees can improve soil health and generate additional income from timber or fruit. This kind of hands-on experience creates a community of practice that motivates others to explore sustainable methods.

Long-Term Relationships

Establishing long-term relationships between small-scale farmers and various support organisations is vital for sustained progress. Organisations that offer ongoing support rather than one-time assistance can significantly impact farmers' ability to transition to sustainable practices. Regular follow-ups and evaluations can help farmers adapt their practices based on evolving challenges and technological advancements.

For example, agricultural extension services can provide regular training sessions and on-site support to troubleshoot problems as they arise. These relationships foster trust and ensure that farmers feel supported throughout the transition process. When farmers know they can count on assistance, they are more likely to experiment with new practices and share their experiences with others.

Investing in research and innovation targeted at sustainable land management practices specific to the region's challenges can lead to the development of effective solutions. For instance, precision farming technologies, efficient irrigation systems, and organic farming methods can enhance productivity while minimising environmental impact.

Ecosystem Services

Recognising and valuing ecosystem services provided by healthy ecosystems is a critical aspect of biodiversity conservation in India. Ecosystem services are the various benefits that humans derive from nature. These include fundamental necessities such as clean water, air purification, and food production, all of which are essential for human survival and well-being.

Healthy ecosystems play a vital role in regulating natural processes that directly impact human life. For instance, forests and wetlands act as natural filters, purifying the air we breathe and the water we drink. Trees and plants absorb carbon dioxide and release oxygen, contributing to the regulation of atmospheric gases and mitigating climate change impacts. Similarly, wetlands store and filter water, reducing the risk of floods and ensuring clean water supplies.

The Role of Healthy Ecosystems in Food Production

Healthy ecosystems play a vital role in food production. They are home to a variety of plant and animal species, and this biodiversity is important for agriculture. One of the most significant aspects of these ecosystems is the presence of pollinators. Pollinators, such as bees and butterflies, are crucial for the reproduction of many crops. They facilitate the pollination process, which is necessary for plants to produce fruits and seeds.

Without pollinators, many of the foods we enjoy would become scarce. For example, fruits like apples, berries, and watermelon need pollination to develop properly. If bees and butterflies were to disappear, many farmers would struggle to grow these crops. This could lead to higher prices and less variety in our diets. It is clear that pollinators are a key component of our food systems.

Another important factor in food production is the quality of the soil. Fertile soils that are rich in organic matter provide the necessary nutrients for healthy plant growth. Healthy soil supports the root systems of plants, allowing them to absorb water and nutrients effectively. Farmers often utilise practices that promote soil health, such as crop rotation and cover cropping, to maintain the fertility of their fields. These practices not only improve soil quality but also help prevent erosion and nutrient runoff.

The relationship between healthy ecosystems and food production is interconnected. When ecosystems are disturbed, whether through pollution or habitat loss, the services they provide can diminish. For instance, if a wetland is drained for development, it can lead to a decline in the local pollinator population. To maintain food security, it is essential to protect and restore these ecosystems. Implementing sustainable farming methods, cutting back on the use of pesticides, and promoting conservation initiatives can all help achieve this.

Moreover, diverse ecosystems contribute to resilience in agriculture. They allow for a variety of crops to be grown, which can reduce the risk of total crop failure. If farmers plant only one type of crop and a disease or pest affects that crop, the entire harvest can be lost. By planting a range of crops, farmers can ensure a more stable food supply. For example, some farmers practice intercropping, where they grow two or more crops in close proximity. This technique can lead to better yields and less reliance on chemical inputs.

In addition to their role in food production, healthy ecosystems also help regulate pests and diseases. Natural predators in these ecosystems can keep pest populations in check, reducing the need for chemical pesticides. For instance, ladybirds can control aphid populations, which are common pests on many crops. By maintaining a balance in the ecosystem, farmers can naturally manage pests while also supporting biodiversity.

The presence of earthworms and microorganisms further improves soil health. These organisms break down organic matter, which enriches the soil. When plants die and decompose, they provide nutrients back to the soil. Farmers can promote these beneficial organisms through practices like composting and reduced tilling. This not only supports healthy plant growth but also contributes to the overall health of the ecosystem.

To support both food production and ecosystem health, it is essential for communities to work together. Local governments can establish policies that protect natural areas and promote sustainable agricultural practices. Educating farmers about the benefits of biodiversity and ecosystem services can lead to more environmentally friendly farming. Workshops and training sessions can help farmers learn how to integrate these practices into their daily routines.

Consumers also play a significant role in supporting healthy ecosystems. By choosing to purchase organic and sustainably sourced foods, individuals can encourage farmers to adopt practices that benefit the environment. Supporting local farmers' markets can foster a closer connection between consumers and producers. This relationship can promote sustainable practices and raise awareness about the importance of healthy ecosystems.

In conclusion, preserving and enhancing healthy ecosystems is essential for successful food production. By protecting the biodiversity within these systems and promoting sustainable agricultural practices, we can ensure a stable and nutritious food supply for future generations. The choices we make today will have a lasting impact on the health of our ecosystems and our ability to feed the growing population.

Furthermore, healthy ecosystems contribute to climate regulation and erosion control. Forests and grasslands act as carbon sinks, absorbing large amounts of carbon dioxide from the atmosphere and storing it in biomass and soil. This process helps mitigate global warming by reducing greenhouse gas concentrations. Additionally, vegetation cover stabilises soil, preventing erosion from wind and water. This is particularly important in areas prone to landslides and desertification, where soil loss can have devastating effects on local communities and economies.

Payment for Ecosystem Services (PES) mechanisms provide economic incentives for conservation activities, encouraging landowners and communities to protect and sustainably manage their natural resources. PES schemes involve financial compensation to individuals or groups who undertake actions that enhance ecosystem services. For example, farmers might receive payments for maintaining forested areas on their land, thereby preserving biodiversity and reducing carbon emissions.

Effective valuation of ecosystem services is crucial for integrating them into economic decision-making. By assigning monetary value to the benefits provided by ecosystems, policymakers and stakeholders can better appreciate their importance and make informed choices about land use and development. Valuation techniques often involve assessing the cost of replacing ecosystem services with artificial alternatives. For instance, calculating the expense of building and maintaining water treatment facilities can underscore the value of natural wetlands in providing clean water.

Engaging in thorough valuation requires comprehensive data collection and analysis.

Ecologists, economists, and other experts must work together to quantify the benefits of ecosystem services accurately. Such interdisciplinary collaboration enables a more holistic understanding of the intricate relationships between ecosystems and human well-being.

Incorporating the value of ecosystem services into national accounting systems and policy frameworks can drive sustainable development. When governments recognise the economic contributions of healthy ecosystems, they are more likely to prioritise conservation efforts. This approach aligns with the principle of "natural capital," which treats ecosystems as valuable assets that need to be preserved and managed responsibly.

Education and public awareness are also essential in promoting the recognition and valuation of ecosystem services. Informing communities about the benefits they receive from nature can foster a sense of stewardship and motivate collective action towards conservation. Outreach programmes, workshops, and educational campaigns can help bridge the gap between scientific knowledge and public perception, empowering individuals to participate in ecosystem management.

Moreover, PES mechanisms can be tailored to address specific conservation goals and local contexts. In regions where deforestation is a major concern, payments could be directed towards reforestation projects and sustainable forestry practices. In agricultural landscapes, incentives might focus on promoting agroecological techniques that enhance biodiversity and soil health. Customising PES schemes to local needs ensures that conservation efforts are both effective and equitable.

To ensure the success of PES mechanisms, transparent monitoring and evaluation are necessary. Regular assessments allow for the tracking of ecological outcomes and the adjustment of strategies as needed. By measuring the impacts of conservation activities, stakeholders can identify best practices and replicate successful models in other areas.

Institutional support is also vital for implementing PES initiatives. Governments, non-governmental organisations (NGOs), and international agencies must collaborate to create enabling environments for PES schemes. This includes establishing legal frameworks, providing technical assistance, and securing funding for long-term sustainability. PES mechanisms have the potential to be important drivers of biodiversity conservation if they receive support from strong institutions.

Evidence from existing PES programmes illustrates their effectiveness in achieving conservation goals. For example, Costa Rica's PES system has successfully restored forest cover and enhanced biodiversity while providing economic benefits to rural communities. Similar schemes in India could yield comparable results, contributing to the country's broader conservation objectives.

Challenges and Call to Action

Addressing the diverse and interconnected challenges to biodiversity conservation in India is critical for maintaining the nation's rich natural heritage. India, with its varied ecosystems ranging from the Himalayan mountains to coastal mangroves, faces several significant threats like habitat loss, climate change, and pollution. Habitat loss, primarily driven by land-use changes such as deforestation and urban sprawl, continues to fragment ecosystems and diminish wildlife populations. Industrialisation and agricultural expansion often lead to this destruction, isolating species and reducing genetic diversity, which compromises their capacity to adapt to environmental shifts. Climate change further exacerbates these pressures by altering temperature and precipitation patterns, disrupting habitats, and forcing species migration. Additionally, pollution from industrial waste, agricultural runoff, and plastic debris contaminates water, soil, and air, affecting plant and animal health and disrupting food chains.

To address these dynamic conservation issues, adaptive management strategies are essential. These strategies involve a continuous process of monitoring, evaluating, and adjusting management actions to respond effectively to changing conditions and new information. For instance, integrated landscape management approaches can buffer against the adverse impacts of habitat fragmentation by promoting connectivity between protected areas and fostering sustainable land-use practices in surrounding landscapes. This helps maintain ecological processes and allows species to migrate and adapt in response to climate change. Restoration ecology practices, such as reforestation and wetland restoration, can also mitigate habitat loss and enhance ecosystem resilience. This responsiveness ensures that conservation efforts remain relevant and effective despite evolving environmental challenges.

Strong political will is a cornerstone for driving meaningful biodiversity conservation initiatives. Governments must prioritise environmental policies, allocate adequate resources, and enforce regulations to protect natural habitats and wildlife. Legislation aimed at regulating land use, controlling pollution, and protecting endangered species needs robust implementation to be effective. Political leaders should champion conservation causes, encouraging public institutions and the private sector to adopt sustainable practices. Moreover, biodiversity considerations should be integrated into broader policy frameworks, including agriculture, urban planning, and economic development, to ensure holistic and supportive measures across various sectors.

Increased public awareness and involvement are equally crucial for successful conservation outcomes. Educational campaigns and outreach programmes can foster a deeper understanding of biodiversity's importance and the threats it faces. Engaging communities through citizen science initiatives, nature clubs, and school programmes can build a culture of conservation at the grassroots level. When people recognise the intrinsic and utilitarian value of biodiversity, they are more likely to support and participate in conservation activities. Additionally, media campaigns highlighting success stories and conservation heroes can inspire collective action and behavioural changes that benefit the environment.

Collaborative efforts among government agencies, non-governmental organisations (NGOs), businesses, and local communities can significantly enhance conservation outcomes. Multisectoral partnerships leverage the strengths and resources of different stakeholders, creating synergies that amplify conservation impacts. Government bodies can provide regulatory frameworks and funding, while NGOs offer expertise in wildlife management and community engagement. Businesses can contribute through corporate social responsibility initiatives, green technologies, and sustainable practices in their operations. Local communities, being the custodians of their environments, bring invaluable traditional knowledge and on-the-ground insights that can guide effective conservation strategies.

For example, joint forest management programmes that involve local communities in decision-making and benefit-sharing have shown promise in sustainably managing forest resources. Similarly, public-private partnerships in eco-tourism can generate revenue for conservation projects and promote environmental education among visitors. Collaborative conservation models that integrate scientific research, policy advocacy, and community participation create a comprehensive approach that addresses both ecological and socio-economic dimensions of biodiversity preservation.

Adaptive management strategies play a vital role in addressing these challenges. With the recognition that ecosystems are dynamic and constantly changing, conservation efforts must be flexible and responsive. An effective adaptive management strategy involves continuous monitoring and assessment of conservation actions and outcomes. This approach allows for informed adjustments based on new data and changing environmental conditions, ensuring that conservation measures remain relevant and effective over time. For instance, periodically reviewing the status of protected areas and updating management plans based on ecological monitoring data can help maintain their effectiveness in preserving biodiversity.

Strong political will is indispensable for driving conservation initiatives forward. Decision-makers must prioritise biodiversity conservation on national agendas and allocate sufficient resources for implementation. Developing and enforcing strict regulations to curb habitat destruction, pollution, and illegal wildlife trade is essential. Furthermore, integrating biodiversity conservation into broader policy frameworks, such as urban planning, agriculture, and industrial development, can ensure that conservation goals are aligned with other developmental objectives.

Public awareness and advocacy are equally crucial in galvanising support for conservation efforts. Educating communities about the importance of biodiversity and the threats it faces can foster a sense of stewardship and responsibility. Campaigns that highlight the ecological, economic, and cultural values of biodiversity can motivate individuals and communities to actively participate in conservation actions. Community-based initiatives, such as citizen science projects and environmental education programmes, empower local populations to contribute to biodiversity monitoring and protection efforts.

Effective biodiversity conservation requires collaborative efforts from multiple stakeholders. Government agencies, non-governmental organisations (NGOs), academic institutions, businesses, and local communities all have important roles to play. Partnerships that leverage the unique strengths and resources of each stakeholder group can result in innovative and impactful conservation solutions. For example, collaborations between scientific researchers and local communities can combine traditional knowledge with modern scientific techniques to develop context-specific conservation strategies. Businesses can adopt sustainable practices and support conservation initiatives through corporate social responsibility programmes.

Final Insights

The chapter has explored various policy frameworks that support biodiversity conservation in India, emphasising the need to balance development with ecological preservation. Key legislative measures such as the Wildlife Protection Act, Forest Conservation Act, and National Biodiversity Act have been highlighted for their significant contributions to protecting India's flora and fauna. The chapter also pointed out the necessity of integrating biodiversity considerations into broader policy domains like agriculture, urban planning, and industrial development to achieve sustainable outcomes.

Furthermore, the role of community involvement in conservation efforts has been underscored. Initiatives like Joint Forest Management and Community Conserved Areas demonstrate how local communities can effectively manage natural resources and enhance biodiversity. By blending traditional knowledge with modern scientific approaches, these community-based strategies contribute to more resilient and adaptive conservation practices. The chapter concludes by recommending actions for better integration of biodiversity objectives into various sectors, emphasising cross-sectoral policies, strong enforcement, public awareness, and enhanced monitoring systems.

Reference List

DeepBlueInk. (2024, March 17). *Indigenous Knowledge and Sustainable Forestry: Honouring Traditional Wisdom for Forest Conservation* . Medium; Medium. https://medium.com/@angelicdolphin12/indigenous-knowledge-and-sustainable-forestry-honoring-traditional-wisdom-for-forest-conservation-4b0e05bbd912

Ecosystem Services | Climate Change Resource Centre . (n.d.). Www.fs.usda.gov. http://www.fs.usda.gov/ccrc/topics/ecosystem-services

Fedele, G., Locatelli, B., & Djoudi, H. (2017, December). *Mechanisms mediating the contribution of ecosystem services to human well-being and resilience* . Ecosystem Services. https://doi.org/10.1016/j.ecoser.2017.09.011

Kumar, A. (2021). *Environmental policy framework in India and biodiversity conservation: Review* . *ResearchGate* . https://www.researchgate.net/publication/356493398_ENVIRONMENTAL_POLICY_FRAMEWORK_IN_INDIA_AND_BIODIVERSITY_CONSERVATION_REVIEW

Keprate, A., Bhardwaj, D. R., Sharma, P., Verma, K., Abbas, G., Sharma, V., Sharma, K., & Shiva Janju. (2024, January 1). *Climate-resilient Resilient systems for Sustainable Land Use and Livelihood* . World Sustainability Series, Springer International Publishing. https://doi.org/ 10.1007/978-3-031-63430-7_7

Sustainable land management | WILDLABS . (n.d.). Wildlabs.net. https://wildlabs.net/article/ sustainable-land-managment

Traditional Knowledge and Conservation of Biodiversity for Sustainable Livelihoods by Tribal Communities in Southern India . (2024). Fao.org. https://www.fao.org/4/xii/0613-b1.htm

The Challenges of Biodiversity Conservation . (n.d.). Www.joesblooms.com. https://

www.joesblooms.com/the-challenges-of-biodiversity-conservation

The Royal Society. (2024). *What is the human impact on biodiversity? | Royal Society* . Royalsociety.org. https://royalsociety.org/news-resources/projects/biodiversity/human-impact-on-biodiversity/

lh-prince. (2024). *Safeguarding India's biodiversity: Wildlife and forest conservation laws . Law Hub* . Retrieved from https://law-hub.in/introduction-to-law/india-wildlife-forest-conservation-laws/

Chapter 7

The Forest of Tigers: People, Politics and Environment in the Sundarbans

Exploring the socio-ecological dynamics of the Sundarbans presents a unique opportunity to understand the intricate relationship between local inhabitants, Bengal tigers, and conservation politics. The Sundarbans, one of the largest mangrove forests in the world, is not just home to diverse wildlife but also supports millions of people who depend on its resources for their livelihoods. This region's complex interplay between human activity and natural habitat offers valuable insights into how societies adapt and coexist with nature amid environmental challenges.

In this chapter, we will delve into various aspects that shape the life and environment of the Sundarbans. We begin by examining the ways local communities interact with their surroundings through activities such as fishing, honey collection, and wood gathering. This interaction often brings them into direct conflict with the wildlife, especially Bengal tigers, leading to a precarious balance between safety and survival. The chapter then explores the political dimensions of conservation efforts, highlighting the tensions between global conservation priorities and local community needs. It will also address human-wildlife conflicts and propose strategies for mitigating these issues while ensuring sustainable coexistence. By analysing the impact of climate change and environmental degradation, we aim to present a comprehensive view of both the ecological and socio-economic challenges facing the Sundarbans.

Overview of the Sundarbans

The Sundarbans, a vast expanse of mangrove forest stretching across India and Bangladesh, stands as the largest such ecosystem in the world. This unique environment is not just an ecological treasure but also a UNESCO World Heritage site due to its incredible biodiversity. The Sundarbans serves as a vital habitat for a range of species, including the iconic Bengal tiger, the formidable saltwater crocodile, and a plethora of bird and fish species. This region's significance extends beyond its natural wonders, supporting millions of people who rely on its resources for their livelihoods.

Understanding the importance of the Sundarbans begins with its sheer scale and complexity. With a total area spanning about 10,000 square kilometres, it is the largest contiguous block of mangrove forest remaining in the world. These mangroves serve as a critical buffer zone, protecting inland areas from the impacts of tropical storms and cyclones, which are frequent in the Bay of Bengal. The dense root systems of the mangroves stabilise the coastline and reduce erosion, playing a crucial role in maintaining the health and stability of coastal regions.

The Sundarbans' designation as a UNESCO World Heritage site underscores its global ecological value. This recognition is due to its role as a biodiversity hotspot, housing numerous endangered and globally significant species. The Bengal tiger, perhaps the most famous inhabitant of this region, exemplifies the delicate balance between predator and prey within this ecosystem. The tigers here have adapted to the harsh saline conditions, displaying unique behaviours not seen in other tiger populations. Alongside tigers, the Sundarbans houses other apex predators like the saltwater crocodile, which further enhances the ecological complexity of this region.

Birdlife in the Sundarbans is equally impressive, with the presence of species such as the brown-winged kingfisher and the masked finfoot, both of which are rare and threatened. The intricate network of rivers, tidal waterways, and mudflats creates varied habitats that support these diverse avian populations, making the region a paradise for ornithologists and bird watchers alike. Additionally, the waters of the Sundarbans teem with fish species that are vital not only to the local food web but also to the millions of people who depend on fishing for their sustenance and economic well-being.

The human dimension of the Sundarbans adds another layer of complexity to its ecological narrative. Over four million people live in the Indian part of the Sundarbans alone, relying heavily on the forest and its resources for their daily needs. Activities such as fishing, honey collection, and agriculture are integral to the livelihoods of these communities. The Sundarbans therefore represents a classic example of a human-nature interface, where socio-economic activities are intricately linked to the health of the ecosystem.

This dependence on natural resources creates unique socio-ecological dynamics. For instance, the practice of honey collection involves venturing deep into tiger territory, exposing local people to potential wildlife conflicts. Despite the dangers, these practices have persisted through generations, reflecting a deep cultural connection to the land and its resources. The interdependency between people and nature in the Sundarbans is a testament to the resilience and adaptability of local communities in the face of environmental challenges.

However, the Sundarbans are not without their threats. Climate change poses significant risks to this delicate ecosystem, with rising sea levels and an increased frequency of severe storms threatening both biodiversity and human settlements. Mangrove degradation due to illegal logging and land conversion for agriculture further exacerbates these vulnerabilities. Effective conservation strategies are essential to safeguarding the ecological integrity of the Sundarbans while ensuring the well-being of the dependent human populations.

Efforts to conserve the Sundarbans must recognise the complexities of this socio-ecological system. Conservation policies need to be inclusive, taking into account the voices and knowledge of local communities that have lived in harmony with this environment for centuries. Initiatives like community-based forest management and sustainable resource use practices are crucial for the long-term preservation of the Sundarbans. By empowering local people and integrating traditional ecological knowledge with modern conservation techniques, it is possible to create a balanced approach that benefits both the environment and human societies.

People and the Environment

The interaction between locals and their environment in the Sundarbans is a complex and multifaceted relationship, driven by the need for survival and shaped by cultural and socio-economic factors. The local communities in this region depend heavily on natural resources for their livelihood. Fishing, honey collection, and wood gathering are among the primary activities that sustain these populations. However, these activities often bring them into direct conflict with the wildlife inhabiting the same space, particularly the Bengal tigers.

Fishing is a critical source of income and food for many local families. The waters of the Sundarbans are rich in fish, crabs, and other aquatic life, providing sustenance to those who brave its challenges. Fishermen venture into crocodile-infested waters and tidal rivers, facing the constant threat of tiger attacks. Restrictions imposed to protect the forest's biodiversity have further complicated matters. Conservation efforts aimed at protecting the tiger population have inadvertently restricted access to fishing zones, exacerbating the vulnerability of these communities (Siddique et al., 2023).

Honey collection is another vital activity. The Sundarbans are known for their dense mangrove forests, home to nectar-rich flowers that attract bees, leading to the production of high-quality honey. Honey collectors, locally known as "Mouals," enter the forest in groups, often staying for several days, to extract honey from beehives. This activity not only poses physical risks from bee stings but also from potential tiger encounters. Tigers may perceive humans as threats or prey, especially when they encroach on the animals' territory during honey collection. The tension between conservation measures and livelihood activities encapsulates a broader struggle where the needs of local communities must be balanced with ecological preservation.

Wood gathering is equally essential for daily survival, providing fuel for cooking and raw materials for construction. The mangroves offer a ready supply of timber, but like fishing and honey collection, wood gathering increases the likelihood of human-tiger conflicts. The presence of people deep within the forest disturbs the natural habitat of tigers, leading to dangerous encounters. The dependence on such activities underscores the precarious balance locals must maintain to coexist with the wildlife around them.

Tigers hold a prominent place in the local culture and beliefs of the Sundarbans inhabitants. These majestic creatures symbolise power, danger, and spirituality. In many ways, the tiger is revered and feared simultaneously. Locally, the term "baghe-dhora" (caught by a tiger) signifies more than just a physical encounter; it carries spiritual connotations, often stigmatising families who experience such tragedies (Chowdhury et al., 2016). The death of a family member due to a tiger attack can lead to social isolation and discrimination against surviving relatives, particularly widows, who are branded as "tiger widows." This stigma impacts their ability to remarry or gain social acceptance, compounding their already dire socio-economic conditions.

Despite the fear and danger associated with tigers, there is also a recognition of their role in maintaining the forest ecosystem. Tigers help regulate the population of herbivores, which in turn helps preserve vegetation. This predator-prey dynamic is crucial for the health of the Sundarbans' diverse ecosystems. Local beliefs often reflect this duality, where tigers are seen as both destroyers and guardians of the forest. This ambivalence towards tigers reveals a deeper understanding of the intricate web of life that sustains the Sundarbans.

The interactions between locals and their environment thus reflect broader socio-economic challenges. The dependence on natural resources coupled with restrictive conservation policies often puts tremendous pressure on the local populations. Poverty and limited access to alternative livelihoods make it difficult for people to move away from traditional practices. Moreover, the enforcement of conservation laws without considering the socio-cultural context of the communities leads to resistance and non-compliance. Effective conservation strategies must therefore be inclusive, taking into account the voices and needs of the local inhabitants to ensure both ecological sustainability and human welfare.

Conservation efforts in the Sundarbans must strive to create a sustainable balance between protecting the unique biodiversity and supporting the aspirations of the local communities. Participatory decision-making processes, involving locals in the planning and implementation of conservation measures, could mitigate some of the conflicts. For instance, introducing community-based ecotourism initiatives or alternate livelihood programmes could provide economic opportunities while reducing dependency on forest resources. By engaging the community in conservation efforts, it becomes possible to foster a sense of ownership and responsibility towards preserving the environment.

The Politics of Conservation

Investigating the political aspects of conservation efforts in the Sundarbans reveals a complex interplay between global conservation priorities and local community needs. Conflicts often arise when international conservation goals, which emphasise wildlife preservation, clash with the resource requirements of local populations who depend heavily on the region for their livelihoods. The Sundarbans are home to both the endangered Bengal tigers and millions of people whose survival activities include fishing, honey collection, and wood gathering. These activities are tightly woven into the socio-economic fabric of the community, making any disruption significant.

Top-down conservation approaches, which are frequently championed by international organisations and governments, have been criticised for displacing local communities. These strategies often involve creating protected areas or imposing restrictions without adequate consultation with the affected populations. The result can be increased poverty, as people lose access to critical resources, and a sense of alienation from their environment. Such displacement not only undermines traditional ways of life but also erodes the social structures that have historically supported sustainable resource use.

Jalais argues for more inclusive conservation strategies, emphasising the need to integrate local voices and knowledge into the conservation process. This bottom-up approach aims to foster a cooperative relationship between conservationists and local communities, ensuring that the latter's needs and insights shape conservation policies. Including local communities in decision-making processes can lead to more sustainable and effective outcomes. For instance, community-based initiatives that leverage indigenous knowledge about the ecosystem can offer innovative solutions to conservation challenges while respecting local traditions and rights.

Recognising and addressing the rights of marginalised communities is essential for the success of conservation efforts. Historically, conservation practices have often overlooked or even violated the rights of indigenous and local communities, leading to tension and resistance. Effective conservation requires a framework that respects these communities' rights to land, resources, and self-determination. This recognition can help build trust and cooperation, making conservation efforts more resilient and adaptable.

One example of this is the successful implementation of community forestry programmes, where local communities manage forest resources under agreed-upon conservation guidelines. These programmes have shown that when communities have a stake in the conservation process, they are more likely to engage in sustainable practices. In the context of the Sundarbans, similar community-driven initiatives could balance tiger conservation with the sustainable use of forest and water resources, providing a model for other regions facing similar challenges.

Human-Wildlife Conflict

Human-tiger conflicts in the Sundarbans arise due to unique ecological conditions where the dense mangrove forest, interspersed with tidal waterways, is home to a significant population of Bengal tigers. These tigers often hunt humans, a behaviour attributed to several factors. In the densely vegetated environment of the Sundarbans, tigers have adapted to a mixed diet that occasionally includes human prey, primarily due to habitat encroachment and the scarcity of their natural prey.

In response to the threat of tiger attacks, local inhabitants have developed various strategies to protect themselves. One well-known method involves wearing masks on the backs of their heads. This practice exploits the tiger's tendency to attack from behind, as the mask gives the impression of constant human vigilance. Additionally, barriers constructed from wooden poles, wire mesh, and nylon netting are employed to prevent tigers from entering villages. Aversive conditioning techniques, such as using electrified 'human dummies,' have also been tested, although their efficacy remains inconclusive (Says, 2011).

The consequences of human-tiger conflict are profound for both humans and tigers. For humans, these encounters often result in fatalities or severe injuries, leading to socio-economic hardships for affected families. Livelihoods are disrupted as fear of tiger attacks restricts activities like fishing and honey collection, crucial for subsistence. Financial compensation for victims' families does offer some relief, but it can never fully mitigate the loss suffered (Says, 2011).

For tigers, human-tiger conflict threatens their survival. Tigers involved in attacks are often killed in retaliation, exacerbating their already vulnerable status. The presence of tigers near human settlements fuels negative perceptions, potentially undermining conservation efforts. Conservationists face the dilemma of balancing the protection of these apex predators while ensuring the safety and livelihoods of local communities.

Broader socio-economic factors further intensify these conflicts. Limited livelihood options and inadequate healthcare services compel locals to venture into tiger-inhabited areas for resources, increasing the likelihood of encounters. The reliance on forest resources for income means that efforts to keep people out of these areas are met with resistance, highlighting the complex interplay between poverty and conservation challenges.

Addressing human-tiger conflict in the Sundarbans requires holistic strategies that consider the socio-economic realities of local communities. Initiatives that provide alternative livelihood opportunities, improve healthcare access, and involve local stakeholders in conservation planning are essential. By integrating the needs and perspectives of the local populace, sustainable coexistence with Bengal tigers becomes more attainable.

Effective conflict mitigation strategies also necessitate ongoing research and adaptive management. Understanding the behavioural ecology of tigers and the spatiotemporal patterns of human activity can inform targeted interventions. For instance, identifying high-risk zones and periods for tiger attacks can help in planning safer times and places for resource collection activities.

Moreover, the promotion of awareness and education programmes within local communities can play a crucial role. Educating people about tiger behaviour, safe practices in tiger habitats, and the importance of tiger conservation fosters a more informed and cooperative approach to managing human-tiger interactions.

Technological advancements also offer promising avenues for mitigating conflicts. The use of GPS collars and camera traps to monitor tiger movements can provide real-time data, enabling timely warnings to communities about tiger proximities. Additionally, community-based surveillance systems that employ local volunteers can enhance early detection and response mechanisms.

The implementation of comprehensive compensation schemes is equally vital. Streamlining the process to ensure prompt and fair compensation for livestock losses and human casualties can alleviate financial burdens and reduce hostility towards tigers. Transparent and efficient compensation mechanisms build trust between communities and conservation authorities, encouraging collaborative efforts.

Relocation of human settlements from critical tiger habitats is another proactive measure. While challenging, successful relocation projects can reduce human-tiger interactions and preserve essential habitats for tigers. Ensuring relocated communities receive adequate support and opportunities can make this strategy more viable and acceptable.

Environmental Degradation and Climate Change

The Sundarbans, a sprawling mangrove forest located at the delta of the Ganges, Brahmaputra, and Meghna rivers on the Bay of Bengal, is experiencing significant environmental challenges. These issues not only threaten the unique biodiversity of the region but also jeopardise the livelihoods of the millions who call this area home.

One of the most pressing environmental challenges in the Sundarbans is the impact of climate change. Rising sea levels pose a severe threat to both the natural ecosystem and human settlements. Over the past few decades, the sea level in the Sundarbans has been rising faster than the global average. This rise, coupled with increased cyclonic activity, has led to frequent and more intense flooding. Such floods devastate communities, destroy habitats, and erode the coastline, leading to a loss of land mass. As the sea encroaches further inland, many islands within the Sundarbans are at risk of disappearing entirely within the next century (Loss and Damage in the Sundarbans, n.d.).

Cyclones, which have become more frequent and severe due to climate change, bring with them immense destruction. The storms ravage infrastructure, uproot trees, and disrupt the delicate balance of the mangrove ecosystem. The local population, primarily dependent on agriculture, fishing, and honey collection, suffers significantly during these events. With homes and livelihoods destroyed, families are often forced to migrate, leaving behind their ancestral lands and traditional means of sustenance (*(PDF) Climate Change: Impact on the Sundarbans: A Case Study*, n.d.).

Environmental degradation exacerbates the challenges posed by climate change. Deforestation, pollution, and unsustainable practices contribute to the vulnerability of the Sundarbans' ecosystem. Illegal logging and timber extraction reduce the dense mangrove cover, weakening the natural barrier against storm surges and reducing the habitat available for wildlife. Pollution from upstream industrial activities and untreated sewage discharge degrades water quality, impacting aquatic life and human health alike. Additionally, unsustainable agricultural practices and overfishing strain natural resources, leading to a decline in fish stocks and soil fertility.

Addressing these multifaceted challenges requires a holistic approach that takes into account social, economic, and political factors. Conservation efforts cannot succeed in isolation; they must incorporate the needs and knowledge of local communities. It's important to recognise that while conservation is crucial, the well-being of the local population should not be compromised. Policies that prioritise environmental preservation without considering socio-economic realities can lead to conflicts and further disenfranchisement of the already vulnerable population.

A sustainable solution would balance environmental conservation with community well-being. This involves promoting livelihood options that are both environmentally friendly and economically viable. For instance, encouraging the cultivation of saline-resistant crops can help farmers maintain their productivity even as salinity levels rise. Similarly, integrating traditional knowledge with modern conservation techniques can ensure that development initiatives are culturally appropriate and scientifically sound.

Furthermore, it is essential to strengthen the institutional framework governing the Sundarbans. Currently, overlapping responsibilities between central and state institutions often lead to inefficiencies and delays in implementation. Establishing a clear and coordinated governance structure can enhance the effectiveness of conservation and development programmes. Additionally, providing adequate financial and technical support to local authorities can empower them to manage the region's resources more sustainably.

Another critical aspect of addressing the environmental challenges in the Sundarbans is fostering community resilience. This involves improving disaster preparedness and response mechanisms. Establishing flood relief centres, creating early warning systems, and training local communities in emergency response can significantly reduce the impact of natural disasters. Moreover, enhancing healthcare and education services can improve the overall quality of life, making communities more resilient to environmental shocks.

Globally, there is an urgent need to mitigate climate change by reducing greenhouse gas emissions. International cooperation and adherence to climate agreements are vital to curbing the adverse effects of climate change. Additionally, developed countries ought to offer financial and technological support to areas like the Sundarbans, which suffer disproportionately from climate change despite making a negligible contribution to its causes.

To protect the Sundarbans from tiger attacks, several actionable steps can be taken. Installing and maintaining boundary fences in high-risk areas can prevent tigers from entering villages. Utilising motion-sensor cameras and alarm systems can alert villagers to the presence of tigers, allowing them to take precautionary measures. Furthermore, organising community awareness programmes and training sessions on safe practices when venturing into tiger habitats can reduce the likelihood of encounters. Equipping field workers with protective gear, such as reinforced boots and helmets, can also minimise injuries in case of an attack. Collaborating with local wildlife experts to develop and implement non-lethal deterrents, such as noise-making devices or scent repellents, can effectively keep tigers at bay without harming them. Finally, establishing rapid response teams to handle tiger-related emergencies ensures swift action to protect both humans and tigers.

Final Insights

The intricate socio-ecological dynamics of the Sundarbans showcase the delicate balance between local communities, their environment, and conservation efforts. The livelihoods of millions rely on activities such as fishing, honey collection, and wood gathering, which bring them into close contact with Bengal tigers and other wildlife. These interactions highlight the necessity for inclusive conservation strategies that address the needs of both humans and the ecosystem. Effective policies must consider traditional practices and knowledge, ensuring that local voices are integral to decision-making processes.

Conservation in the Sundarbans faces challenges from climate change and environmental degradation, threatening both biodiversity and human settlements. Rising sea levels and increased cyclonic activity exacerbate vulnerabilities, while illegal logging and pollution further strain natural resources. Sustainable solutions require a balanced approach, integrating community well-being with ecological preservation. Strengthening governance structures, promoting resilient livelihoods, and fostering international cooperation are key to mitigating these threats. By aligning conservation priorities with socio-economic realities, we can work towards a sustainable future for the Sundarbans and their inhabitants.

Reference List

Armitage, D., Mbatha, P., Muhl, E., Rice, W., & Sowman, M. (2020, January 8). *Governance principles for community-centred conservation in the post-2020 global biodiversity framework* . Conservation Science and Practice. https://doi.org/10.1111/csp2.160

Chowdhury, A., Brahma, A., Mondal, R., & Biswas, M. (2016). *Stigma of tiger attack: Study of tiger-widows from Sundarban Delta, IndiaFNx01* . Indian Journal of Psychiatry. https://doi.org/10.4103/0019-5545.174355

Esmail, N., McPherson, J. M., Abulu, L., Amend, T., Amit, R., Bhatia, S., Bikaba, D., Brichieri-Colombi, T. A., Brown, J., Buschman, V., Fabinyi, M., Farhadinia, M., Ghayoumi, R., Hay-Edie, T., Horigue, V., Jungblut, V., Jupiter, S., Keane, A.,

Macdonald, D. W., & Mahajan, S. L. (2023, March 17). *What's on the horizon for community-based conservation? Emerging threats and opportunities* . Trends in Ecology and Evolution. https://doi.org/10.1016/j.tree.2023.02.008

Loss and Damage in the Sundarbans . (n.d.). Zero Carbon Analytics: https://zerocarbon-analytics.org/archives/justice/loss-and-damage-in-the-sundarbans

(PDF) Climate Change: Impact on the Sundarbans: A case study . (n.d.). ResearchGate. https://www.researchgate.net/publication/311607858_Climate_Change_-_Impact_on_the_Sundarbans_A_case_study

Sarker, S. K., Reeve, R., Paul, N. K., & Matthiopoulos, J. (2019, January 10). *Modelling spatial biodiversity in the world's largest* mangrove ecosystem—The Bangladesh Sundarbans: A baseline for conservation (F. Essl, Ed.). Diversity and Distributions. https://doi.org/10.1111/ddi.12887

Says, S. (2011, March 4). *Human-Tiger conflict: Cause, Consequence and Mitigation* . Conservation India. https://www.conservationindia.org/articles/human-tiger-conflict-cause-consequence-and-mitigation

Sievers, M., Chowdhury, M. R., Adame, M. F., Bhadury, P., Bhargava, R., Buelow, C., Friess, D. A., Ghosh, A., Hayes, M. A., McClure, E. C., Pearson, R. M., Turschwell, M. P., Worthington, T. A., & Connolly, R. M. (2020, November 1). *Indian Sundarbans mangrove forest considered endangered under Red List of Ecosystems, but there is cause for optimism* . Biological Conservation. https://doi.org/10.1016/j.biocon.2020.108751

Dr. Anthonysamy David

Siddique, M. R. H., Hossain, M., & Rashid, A. Z. M. M. (2023, March). *The dilemma of prioritising conservation over livelihoods: Assessing the impact of fishing restriction to the fishermen of the Sundarbans* . Trees, Forests and People. https://doi.org/10.1016/j.tfp.2022.100366

Sarbendu Bikash Dhar & Mondal, S. (2023, June 1). *Nature of human-tiger conflict in Indian Sundarban* . Trees, Forests and People; Elsevier BV. https://doi.org/10.1016/j.tfp.2023.100401

Chapter 8

Biogeography and Biodiversity in India

Biogeography and biodiversity in India encompass an intricate tapestry of ecosystems and species that highlight the country's vast natural wealth. From the tropical rainforests to the cold Himalayan regions, India offers a unique geographical and climatic range that supports diverse habitats and life forms. This chapter delves into the scientific study of biogeography, exploring how historical and current processes such as plate tectonics, speciation, and climate variations have shaped the distribution of species and ecosystems across the subcontinent. Understanding these elements is essential for appreciating India's role in global biodiversity conservation.

Dr. Anthonysamy David

In this chapter, readers will gain a comprehensive overview of India's distinct ecological zones and their respective biodiversity. The chapter covers various biomes, including tropical rainforests, dry deciduous forests, and arid deserts, each hosting unique flora and fauna. It also examines the critical role of the Himalayas in supporting cold-climate species and regulating regional climate. Special attention is given to India's status as one of the world's megadiverse countries, emphasising areas rich in endemic species and those threatened by human activities. Conservation challenges and strategies, such as habitat loss and climate change, will be scrutinised to offer insights into ongoing efforts to protect India's invaluable biodiversity.

Overview of Biogeography in India

Biogeography is the study of the distribution of species and ecosystems in geographic space and through geological time. This scientific field is pivotal for understanding how different species and ecosystems are interrelated and distributed across various regions of the world. Biogeography provides insights into the historical and current processes that shape the diversity and richness of life on Earth, such as speciation, extinction, plate tectonics, and climatic variations. Understanding biogeography is essential for biodiversity conservation, as it helps identify areas that are rich in species but also vulnerable to threats like habitat destruction and climate change.

India's geographical position significantly contributes to its remarkable biodiversity. Situated at the confluence of three major biogeographic realms—the Palearctic, the Indo-Malayan, and the Afro-tropical—India offers a unique blend of species from these diverse regions. The country's wide latitudinal range, spanning from the humid tropics in the south to the temperate zones of the Himalayas in the north, creates diverse climatic conditions that support various habitats. Additionally, India's topographical features, such as the Western and Eastern Ghats, the Indo-Gangetic plains, the Thar Desert, and the Himalayan mountain range, further enhance its ecological diversity.

The range of habitats found in India is extensive, encompassing everything from lush rainforests to arid deserts. In the north-eastern states, tropical rainforests teem with an incredible variety of flora and fauna. These forests are some of the most biodiverse areas in the country, hosting numerous endemic species. Moving westward, the landscape transitions into the dry deciduous forests of central India, which are home to species like tigers, leopards, and various deer species. The Thar Desert in Rajasthan represents another extreme, where life has adapted to harsh, arid conditions. Despite the challenging environment, this desert hosts unique species like the Great Indian Bustard and the Indian Gazelle. Further south, the Western Ghats, recognised as one of the world's biodiversity hotspots, feature evergreen forests that are a haven for endemic species, including the Nilgiri Tahr and the Malabar Giant Squirrel.

The Himalayan region, often termed as the "Third Pole," plays a crucial role in regulating the climate and hydrology of Asia. The Himalayas harbour a unique array of species adapted to cold climates, such as the Snow Leopard, Red Panda, and Himalayan Monal. This region is also a repository of medicinal plants, many of which are endemic and have significant traditional and economic value. The high altitudes and varied topography create microclimates that support diverse ecosystems within short distances, making the Himalayas a vital area for biodiversity.

India's status as one of the world's 17 megadiverse countries underscores its global importance in biodiversity conservation. Megadiverse countries are those that harbour the majority of Earth's species and high numbers of endemic species. India hosts over 45,500 plant species and 91,000 animal species, accounting for about 7% of all known species globally (India as a Mega Diversity Region, 2024). The country's eight main floristic zones—Western and Eastern Himalayas, Malabar, Assam, the Deccan, Indus and Ganges, and the Andaman Islands—are hotspots of botanical diversity, each supporting a unique assemblage of plant species.

Dr. Anthonysamy David

The Western Ghats, Indo-Burma region, Sundaland, and the Himalayas are recognised as biodiversity hotspots within India, housing a significant portion of the country's endemic plants and animals (Gaurab Nandi Das et al., 2023).

These biodiversity hotspots are not just regions of high species richness; they also face severe threats from human activities. Habitat loss due to deforestation, agricultural expansion, urbanisation, and infrastructure development poses a significant risk to the survival of many species. Climate change further exacerbates these threats by altering habitats and the availability of resources that species depend on. Conservation efforts in these areas are crucial for maintaining the ecological balance and ensuring the survival of endangered species. Protected areas, wildlife sanctuaries, and national parks play a vital role in conserving these critical habitats.

India's commitment to biodiversity conservation is reflected in its policy measures and international commitments. The country is a signatory to various international treaties and conventions aimed at protecting biodiversity, such as the Convention on Biological Diversity (CBD) and the Ramsar Convention on Wetlands. National policies, like the Wildlife Protection Act of 1972 and the Biological Diversity Act of 2002, provide a legal framework for the protection and management of biodiversity. Community involvement and sustainable development practices are also emphasised to ensure that conservation efforts are inclusive and effective.

Ecosystems and Their Biodiversity

India's rich tapestry of ecosystems is a testament to its geographical diversity and climatic variations. This section delves into the specific ecosystems of India, each with unique characteristics and species that highlight the country's unparalleled natural heritage.

Dr. Anthonysamy David

Tropical Rainforests and Their Rich Species Diversity

Tropical rainforests in India are predominantly found in the Western Ghats and the north-eastern states. These forests are characterised by high rainfall, typically exceeding 200 cm annually, which supports a dense canopy of trees reaching heights of up to 60 metres or more. The biodiversity within these ecosystems is astounding; they house a multitude of plant and animal species, many of which are endemic or rare.

These rainforests are home to towering teak, rosewood, and ebony trees. The undergrowth is lush with ferns, orchids, and various types of mosses. Animal life is equally varied and includes several species of birds like hornbills and kingfishers, mammals such as leopards and elephants, and a plethora of insects and reptiles. The presence of these species plays a crucial role in maintaining ecological balance and supporting the local climate.

Unique Cold Climate Species in the Himalayan Ecosystems

The Himalayan range, stretching across the northern frontier of India, encompasses several distinct ecological zones due to its extensive altitudinal range. The higher altitudes feature alpine meadows and tundra, which host cold-resistant species such as the snow leopard, Himalayan tahr, and blue sheep. Vegetation in these regions includes rhododendrons, junipers, and various grasses adapted to the cold and often arid conditions.

Temperate forests dominate the mid-altitudes and include broadleaf and coniferous trees, such as oaks, pines, and firs. These areas are also home to numerous bird species, like the monal pheasant and tragopan. Lower elevations feature subtropical forests with deciduous trees and are rich in biodiversity, housing species such as the red panda and black bear. These ecosystems are vital for their role in water regulation, climate stabilisation, and as habitats for unique flora and fauna.

Dr. Anthonysamy David

Life in Desert Ecosystems Like the Thar Desert

The Thar Desert, located in the northwest of India, represents an ecosystem defined by aridity and extreme temperature fluctuations. Despite the harsh conditions, this desert supports a diverse array of life forms. Flora in the Thar includes drought-resistant plants like cacti, acacias, and thorny shrubs, which have evolved to conserve water efficiently.

The fauna in the Thar Desert is equally remarkable. Adapted to the environment, animals such as the Indian gazelle (chinkara), desert fox, and the critically endangered Great Indian Bustard navigate the sandy terrain with ease. Insects, reptiles, and small mammals form significant parts of the food web, demonstrating nature's resilience and adaptability.

Human settlements in the Thar have also adapted to the challenging environment. Traditional practices of water conservation, such as the construction of step wells and earthen dams, underscore the symbiotic relationship between humans and the desert ecosystem. Overall, the Thar Desert highlights how life can thrive in even the most unyielding environments.

Important Marine Ecosystems Like Mangrove Forests and Coral Reefs

India's extensive coastline, including two major island groups, supports critical marine ecosystems such as mangrove forests and coral reefs. Mangroves, primarily found in the Sundarbans in West Bengal and the Andaman and Nicobar Islands, are specialised coastal woodlands adapted to saline conditions. They play an essential role in coastal protection against erosion and storm surges, sequestering carbon, and providing habitat for numerous aquatic and terrestrial species.

Mangrove species like Rhizophora and Avicennia exhibit unique adaptations such as pneumatophores—specialised roots that enable them to breathe in waterlogged soils. These forests support rich biodiversity, including fish, crustaceans, migratory birds, and the iconic Bengal tiger in the Sundarbans. They also serve as nurseries for many marine species, highlighting their ecological importance.

Coral reefs, especially around the Lakshadweep, Andaman, and Nicobar Islands, are another cornerstone of India's marine biodiversity. These underwater ecosystems are hotspots of marine life, hosting countless species of fish, molluscs, echinoderms, and corals. The vibrant colours and structural complexity of coral reefs make them not only biodiverse but also critical for marine tourism and fisheries.

Coral reefs act as natural barriers against wave action and coastal erosion, thus protecting shorelines. However, they are extremely sensitive to environmental changes, particularly ocean acidification and rising sea temperatures. Conservation efforts are vital to preserving these fragile ecosystems, ensuring that they continue to provide ecological, economic, and cultural benefits.

Conclusion

Biodiversity Hotspots

India's biodiversity hotspots are critical to the global ecosystem due to their unique combination of species richness and endemism. Two such key hotspots in India are the Western Ghats and the Eastern Himalayas, both vital for biodiversity conservation.

The Western Ghats, also known as Sahyadri, stretch for over 1,600 kilometres along the western coast of India. Recognised as one of the world's eight 'hottest hotspots' of biological diversity, this region is home to an estimated 7,402 species of flowering plants, 139 mammal species, 508 bird species, 179 amphibian species, 6,000 insect species, and 290 freshwater fish species. Notably, it hosts a significant percentage of India's terrestrial biodiversity. Many species found here are endemic, meaning they are native to this region alone and not naturally found elsewhere. For instance, the

Nilgiri Tahr, Lion-tailed Macaque, and Malabar Large-spotted Civet are some of the many species that rely on the unique climates and ecosystems provided by the Western Ghats.

Similarly, the Eastern Himalayas extend from Nepal through Bhutan and into northeastern India, encompassing parts of West Bengal, Sikkim, Arunachal Pradesh, and Assam. This range experiences diverse climatic conditions that support a wide variety of habitats, from subtropical forests to alpine meadows. The Eastern Himalayas boast approximately 10,000 species of plants, of which more than 3,000 are endemic. Furthermore, it provides habitat for iconic fauna such as the Red Panda, Snow Leopard, Himalayan Monal, and several species of rhododendrons. The region's endemism is extraordinarily high; many species have evolved in isolation, adapting to the unique environmental conditions offered by these mountainous terrains.

One of the most compelling reasons for protecting these biodiversity hotspots is their high levels of species richness and endemism. Species richness refers to the number of different species represented in an ecological community, landscape, or region. Endemism means that these species are restricted to a particular geographic location, often because of unique environmental conditions. This combination creates ecosystems with high genetic diversity, contributing to the resilience and stability of these environments. These regions act as reservoirs of genetic diversity, crucial for adaptive responses to environmental changes and potential sources of new food crops, pharmaceuticals, and other resources.

However, these regions face significant conservation challenges. Deforestation, agricultural expansion, urbanisation, and infrastructure development are perhaps the main causes of habitat loss. In the Western Ghats, large-scale deforestation has occurred due to commercial logging, plantations (especially tea, coffee, and rubber), and hydroelectric projects. Similarly, the Eastern Himalayas face threats from timber extraction, shifting agriculture, and infrastructural developments like roads and dams.

Climate change further exacerbates these challenges. Rising temperatures and changing precipitation patterns can alter habitats, making them unsuitable for some species while creating opportunities for others. In the Himalayas, for example, the melting of glaciers due to global warming poses a severe threat to species dependent on cold environments. The regional rate of climate warming in the Himalayas is observed to be higher than the global average, leading to the potential extinction of native flora and fauna. Additionally, climate-induced events like landslides and floods can dramatically alter landscapes, resulting in habitat fragmentation and loss.

The need for targeted conservation efforts in these regions cannot be overstated. Conservation strategies should include protected areas, community-based conservation programmes, and sustainable land-use practices. Establishing and effectively managing protected areas is fundamental to safeguarding biodiversity. According to the Convention on Biological Diversity, achieving at least 17% coverage of terrestrial and inland water areas under protection is essential. However, many of India's hotspots fall short of this target, emphasising the need for increased investment in land protection.

Community involvement is also crucial for successful conservation. Local communities often possess intricate knowledge about their environment and play a pivotal role in conservation efforts. Community-based initiatives that integrate traditional knowledge with modern conservation techniques can lead to more sustainable outcomes. For instance, promoting agroforestry and sustainable agricultural practices can help mitigate habitat destruction while providing livelihoods for local populations.

Additionally, there is a pressing need for comprehensive scientific research to guide conservation actions. Detailed studies on species distributions, population dynamics, and ecological interactions within these hotspots can provide insights necessary for effective management. Remote sensing technologies and Geographic Information Systems (GIS) can aid in monitoring habitat changes and identifying critical areas for intervention. Given the complex interplay between various factors driving biodiversity loss, adopting a holistic approach to conservation is essential.

Species Diversity

India's rich and diverse flora and fauna constitute one of the most captivating aspects of its natural heritage. The country's unique geographical position, spanning multiple climatic zones, makes it home to an astounding variety of plant and animal species.

India is a treasure trove of plant diversity, with an estimated 18,000 species of flowering plants. A significant number of these are endemic, meaning they are found nowhere else in the world. India's endemic plants include many that possess medicinal properties and are used in traditional health practices such as Ayurveda, Siddha, and Unani. According to Source 1, India houses about 7,500 species of medicinal plants, accounting for around 44% of the total plant species in the country (Chen et al., 2016). These plants not only form an integral part of cultural traditions but also offer potential pharmaceutical benefits, making their conservation paramount.

The diversity of India's plant life extends beyond medicinal species. The country is home to various ecosystems, ranging from tropical rainforests to alpine tundras, each supporting distinct plant communities. For instance, the Western Ghats and Eastern Himalayas are recognised as global biodiversity hotspots due to their high levels of plant endemism. These regions harbour numerous rare and endangered plant species, which play critical roles in maintaining ecological balance and providing resources for local communities.

India's fauna is equally diverse, comprising more than 90,000 species of animals. This includes over 1,250 bird species, 500 mammal species, and tens of thousands of insect species. The Indian subcontinent is home to some of the world's most iconic wildlife, such as the Bengal tiger, Asiatic lion, Indian elephant, and one-horned rhinoceros. These large mammals occupy varied habitats, from the dense forests of the Sundarbans to the grassy plains of Kaziranga National Park.

In addition to these charismatic megafauna, India also hosts a remarkable variety of lesser-known species. For example, the Western Ghats alone support over 500 species of birds, 219 species of amphibians, and 179 species of reptiles. Many of these species are endemic and have evolved unique adaptations to their environments. Amphibians like the Malabar gliding frog and reptiles like the Indian rock python exemplify the region's rich biodiversity.

Endemic species hold particular importance within India's ecosystem. They often possess specialised roles that contribute significantly to the stability and function of their habitats. For instance, the Nilgiri tahr, a mountain goat found exclusively in the Western Ghats, plays a vital role in maintaining the grassland ecosystem by grazing on specific plant species, thereby preventing overgrowth and promoting plant diversity. Similarly, the lion-tailed macaque, another Western Ghats endemic, aids in seed dispersal, helping to regenerate forest growth.

The conservation of India's endemic species is crucial, given their restricted distributions and specialised habitat requirements. Climate change, illegal poaching, and habitat destruction are all threatening many of these species. Conserving them requires targeted strategies that address these threats while fostering sustainable development.

Habitat loss due to urbanisation, agriculture, and infrastructure development is one of the main conservation issues in India. For example, deforestation for timber and agricultural expansion have greatly diminished the forest cover in several biodiversity-rich areas. Conservation efforts must prioritise the protection of remaining habitats through the establishment and management of protected areas such as national parks, wildlife sanctuaries, and biosphere reserves. As Source 2 indicates, several plant species in India are critically endangered or vulnerable due to habitat destruction and other anthropogenic factors (Gowthami et al., 2021).

Another significant threat to India's biodiversity is climate change, which can alter the delicate balance of ecosystems and render habitats unsuitable for many species. Rising temperatures, changing precipitation patterns, and an increased frequency of extreme weather events pose risks to both plant and animal life. Adaptive management strategies, such as creating corridors that connect fragmented habitats and facilitating species migration, are essential for mitigating the impacts of climate change.

Overexploitation of resources, particularly due to illegal hunting and trade, poses an additional challenge. Iconic species like the Bengal tiger and Indian elephant are often targeted for their skin, bones, and tusks. Strengthening law enforcement and increasing community engagement in conservation efforts are critical steps in combating wildlife crime. Local communities can be empowered to protect their natural heritage through education, alternative livelihood programmes, and participatory conservation initiatives.

Conservation strategies should also incorporate both in-situ and ex-situ approaches. In situ conservation involves protecting species in their natural habitats, whereas ex situ conservation involves breeding and maintaining species in controlled environments such as botanical gardens, zoos, and seed banks. Both methods are complementary and necessary for comprehensive biodiversity conservation.

Conservation Challenges and Strategies

India, known for its rich biodiversity and unique ecosystems, faces significant threats to its natural wealth. Among these, habitat destruction and climate change stand out as two of the most pressing issues. Habitat destruction occurs due to deforestation, urban expansion, and agricultural activities, which lead to the loss of critical habitats for many species. Forests, wetlands, and grasslands are being converted for human use, resulting in fragmented habitats that can no longer support biodiversity as effectively. This not only endangers species but also disrupts ecological processes.

Climate change, on the other hand, is altering weather patterns, temperatures, and precipitation levels, which impacts ecosystems and species distributions. The changing climate exacerbates the effects of habitat destruction by creating conditions that can be unsuitable for many species. For instance, rising temperatures and erratic rainfall patterns affect plant phenology and animal behaviours, leading to mismatches in the timing of biological events such as flowering, migration, and breeding. These changes challenge the survival of species already under pressure from habitat loss.

To address these threats, protected areas play a vital role in conserving biodiversity. India's network of protected areas, which includes national parks, wildlife sanctuaries, and biosphere reserves, provides refuges where species and ecosystems can thrive without direct human interference. These areas serve as conservation hotspots, maintaining ecological integrity and offering a safe haven for endangered species. Effective management of protected areas involves regular monitoring, anti-poaching measures, and habitat restoration projects, ensuring that they continue to support diverse life forms.

However, issues like insufficient funding, understaffed staffing, and encroachment by local communities frequently hamper the effectiveness of protected areas. To overcome these challenges, it is essential to implement guidelines that enhance management practices. Establishing clear boundaries, enhancing patrolling efforts, and involving local communities in conservation initiatives are key steps. Community involvement, in particular, fosters a sense of ownership and responsibility towards conservation goals, leading to more sustainable outcomes.

Sustainable development is another crucial strategy for addressing biodiversity loss. Promoting economic growth while ensuring the conservation of natural resources requires a delicate balance. Sustainable agriculture, responsible forestry, and eco-friendly tourism practices are examples of how development can coexist with biodiversity conservation. For instance, adopting agroforestry systems that integrate trees with crops can improve soil health, increase carbon sequestration, and provide habitat for wildlife, all while supporting local livelihoods.

Community involvement is integral to sustainable development. Engaging local communities in conservation efforts not only empowers them but also leverages their traditional knowledge and practices. Participatory approaches, such as community-managed forests and conservation education programmes, build awareness and encourage sustainable resource use. When communities understand the importance of biodiversity and feel invested in its preservation, they are more likely to adopt practices that benefit both their well-being and the environment.

Key policies and legislation also play a significant role in biodiversity conservation. India has enacted several laws aimed at protecting its natural heritage, such as the Wildlife Protection Act of 1972 and the Forest Conservation Act of 1980. These policies provide a legal framework for establishing protected areas, regulating the use of forest resources, and penalising illegal activities like poaching and logging. Moreover, international agreements, such as the Convention on Biological Diversity (CBD), further reinforce the country's commitment to global conservation goals.

Effective implementation of these policies requires continuous monitoring and adaptation. Regular assessments of policy impact, coupled with scientific research, ensure that legislative measures remain relevant and effective in addressing emerging threats. Additionally, integrating biodiversity considerations into broader policy sectors, such as agriculture, urban planning, and climate change mitigation, helps create a cohesive approach to conservation.

For example, incorporating biodiversity conservation into land-use planning can prevent habitat fragmentation and promote connectivity between protected areas. Similarly, including biodiversity targets in climate action plans ensures that efforts to mitigate climate change also support ecosystem resilience. Cross-sectoral collaboration among government agencies, non-governmental organisations, and academic institutions is crucial for achieving these integrated outcomes.

Insights and Implications

This chapter has provided a thorough examination of India's diverse ecosystems and the unique species that inhabit them. From the tropical rainforests of the Western Ghats and north-eastern states to the arid landscapes of the Thar Desert, each ecosystem supports a remarkable variety of flora and fauna. The critical roles played by regions like the Himalayas in climate regulation and biodiversity preservation have been highlighted, underscoring the complex interplay between geographical features and ecological richness.

The significance of India's biodiversity extends beyond its national boundaries, making the conservation of these ecosystems a global priority. Challenges such as habitat destruction, climate change, and human encroachment pose significant threats to this biodiversity. Effective conservation strategies, including the establishment of protected areas and community involvement, are essential for maintaining the ecological balance. This chapter underscores the need for comprehensive research, sustainable practices, and robust policies to ensure the long-term preservation of India's natural heritage.

Reference List

Chen, S.-L., Yu, H., Luo, H.-M., Wu, Q., Li, C.-F., & Steinmetz, A. (2016, July 30). *Conservation and sustainable use of medicinal plants: problems, progress, and prospects* . Chinese Medicine. https://doi.org/10.1186/s13020-016-0108-7

Gaurab Nandi Das, Zdenek Faltynek Fric, Shristee Panthee, Jatishwor Singh Irungbam, & Konvicka,

M. (2023, June 13). *Geography of Indian Butterflies: Patterns Revealed by Checklists of Federal States* . Insects; Multidisciplinary Digital Publishing Institute. https://doi.org/10.3390/insects14060549

Gowthami, R., Sharma, N., Pandey, R., & Agrawal, A. (2021, May 25). *Status and consolidated list of threatened medicinal plants of India* . Genetic Resources and Crop Evolution. https://doi.org/10.1007/s10722-021-01199-0

GeeksforGeeks. (2023, September 11). *Biodiversity Hotspots in India* . GeeksforGeeks; GeeksforGeeks. https://www.geeksforgeeks.org/biodiversity-hotspots-in-india/

India as a Mega Diversity Region . (2024, June 11). Unacademy. https://unacademy.com/content/

neet-ug/study-material/biology/india-as-a-mega-diversity-region/

India and Its Biodiversity: Ecosystems in India . (n.d.). Indo-Germanbiodiversity.com. http://indo-germanbiodiversity.com/children-segment/ecosystems-in-india.php

India's biodiversity hotspots face climate change challenges . (2014, February 17). Nature India. https://doi.org/10.1038/nindia.2014.21

R.A. Israel Jebasingh, IAS. (2024, August 12). *ECOSYSTEMS OF INDIA* . Blogspot.com. http://officersiasacademy.blogspot.com/2016/03/ecosystems-of-india.html

Chapter 9

The Complexity of Biodiversity

Understanding the complexity of biodiversity is essential, as it encapsulates the intricate variability and variety of life forms on Earth. This diversity ranges from the smallest microorganisms to the largest mammals and encompasses the complex interactions between these life forms within their ecosystems. These interconnections form the foundation of ecosystem stability, resilience, and function, making biodiversity a critical subject for study and conservation. By delving into the numerous facets that contribute to biodiversity, researchers can better appreciate its significance and the intricate balance that maintains ecological health.

In this chapter, we will explore the multifaceted aspects that contribute to the complexity of biodiversity. We will begin by examining the origins of biodiversity through evolutionary processes, including natural selection and speciation. We will also discuss the various adaptive strategies organisms use to survive in diverse environments. Additionally, the chapter will address the significant threats to biodiversity, such as habitat destruction, climate change, pollution, and invasive species. Conservation efforts aimed at mitigating these threats and promoting sustainable practices will be analysed. Furthermore, we will investigate the profound impact humans have on biodiversity and the role they play in both contributing to and combating its decline. Through an objective and technical lens, this chapter aims to provide a comprehensive understanding of biodiversity's complexity and the imperative need for its preservation to maintain ecological and human well-being.

Dr. Anthonysamy David

The Importance of Biodiversity

Biodiversity, the variety and variability of life on Earth, is fundamental to the stability and resilience of ecosystems. It encompasses all forms of life, including plants, animals, microorganisms, and the complex interactions they form within their environments. This diversity forms the backbone of ecosystem function, providing essential services and contributing to human well-being.

Firstly, biodiversity is crucial at the foundational level of ecosystem stability and resilience. Diverse ecosystems are more capable of withstanding environmental stresses and disturbances. For instance, a forest with a wide range of tree species can better resist diseases, pests, and extreme weather events compared to a monoculture plantation. When one species in an ecosystem declines or faces extinction, others can fulfil its ecological roles, thereby maintaining the overall system's functionality. This redundancy ensures that ecosystem processes such as nutrient cycling, water filtration, and soil formation continue unabated, underpinning the health and productivity of the environment (Centre for Biological Diversity, 2019).

Another key aspect of biodiversity is the intricate web of interdependence among species. Each organism plays a specific role in its ecosystem, often forming symbiotic relationships. For example, pollinators like bees and butterflies are vital for the reproduction of flowering plants, which in turn provide food and habitat for various other species. These interconnected networks mean that changes affecting one species can have cascading effects throughout the entire ecosystem. The loss of a single species can disrupt these interactions, leading to broader ecological consequences and potentially triggering further losses. This complexity underscores the importance of conserving not just individual species but the relationships that sustain ecosystem health.

Moreover, organisms contribute significantly to maintaining environmental balance. Predators help control prey populations, preventing overgrazing and allowing vegetation to thrive. Plants produce oxygen through photosynthesis and sequester carbon dioxide, mitigating the effects of climate change. Decomposers like fungi and bacteria break down organic matter, recycling nutrients back into the soil, which supports plant growth. These roles highlight how each species, regardless of its size or perceived importance, contributes to the intricate balance of natural systems. Effective conservation strategies must therefore aim to preserve a wide range of species and their functions to maintain ecological balance.

High biodiversity also delivers critical ecosystem services that are indispensable for human survival. Ecosystem services refer to the benefits humans derive from nature, including provisioning services like food, clean water, and raw materials; regulating services such as climate regulation, pest control, and disease mitigation; supporting services like nutrient cycling and soil formation; and cultural services that provide recreational, aesthetic, and spiritual benefits. For example, diverse agricultural systems are more productive and resilient, ensuring food security by reducing dependency on a limited number of crops. Biodiversity also supports medicinal discoveries, with many current pharmaceuticals derived from natural compounds found in plants and animals. Conservation of biodiversity thus directly translates to safeguarding these vital services upon which human societies depend (Biodiversity: Understanding Its Significance and Conservation, Nature and Culture International, 2024).

In addition to these tangible benefits, biodiversity holds intrinsic value and contributes to cultural richness. From ancient civilisations to modern societies, human cultures have always drawn inspiration from the natural world. Biodiversity enriches our languages, art, literature, and religious practices. It fosters a sense of connection to nature, promotes mental well-being, and enhances our quality of life. Protecting biodiversity is not just about preserving resources but also about maintaining the natural heritage that shapes our cultural identities.

The need for biodiversity conservation is further underscored by the severe consequences of biodiversity loss. Human activities such as deforestation, urbanisation, pollution, and climate change are driving unprecedented rates of species extinction. This loss undermines ecosystem resilience, reduces nature's ability to provide essential services, and exacerbates global environmental challenges. Conservation efforts must therefore prioritise both the protection of high-biodiversity areas, known as hotspots, and the restoration of degraded ecosystems to rebuild their functional integrity.

Efforts to conserve biodiversity should be guided by the recognition that different ecosystems provide unique services and support distinct species assemblages. Tropical rainforests, for instance, are incredibly biodiverse and play a crucial role in climate regulation and carbon sequestration. Coastal mangroves protect shorelines from erosion, support fisheries, and act as nurseries for marine life. Grasslands and savannas sustain large herbivore populations and serve as important carbon sinks. By understanding the specific contributions of various ecosystems, conservation strategies can be tailored to address regional priorities and maximise ecological and socio-economic benefits.

Importantly, effective biodiversity conservation requires a multi-faceted approach involving local communities, governments, scientists, and international organisations. Collaborative efforts can enhance the effectiveness of conservation initiatives by integrating traditional knowledge, scientific research, and policy frameworks. For instance, community-based conservation programmes empower local people to manage and protect their natural resources sustainably. Protected areas, wildlife corridors, and habitat restoration projects help preserve critical ecosystems and species. International agreements and conventions, such as the Convention on Biological Diversity, facilitate global cooperation and resource mobilisation for conservation actions.

Dr. Anthonysamy David

The Origins of Biodiversity

Evolutionary processes are the engine behind the vast and intricate tapestry of biodiversity we see on Earth today. Among these processes, evolution through natural selection plays a pivotal role in shaping diverse life forms. Natural selection operates on the premise that individuals with advantageous traits are more likely to survive and reproduce, passing these traits on to subsequent generations. Over time, this leads to the adaptation of species to their environments and the development of new characteristics that enhance survival and reproductive success.

A classic example of natural selection can be observed in Darwin's finches on the Galápagos Islands. These birds exhibit a variety of beak shapes and sizes, each adapted to specific food sources available on different islands. Finches with beak shapes best suited for the available food types were more likely to thrive and reproduce. As a result, distinct populations evolved unique adaptations, demonstrating how natural selection can drive diversification within a species.

Speciation events are another crucial factor contributing to the proliferation of species. Speciation occurs when populations of a single species become isolated from one another, leading to genetic divergence over time. This isolation can be geographic, behavioural, or ecological. When isolated populations accumulate enough genetic differences, they can no longer interbreed, resulting in the emergence of new species. The evolutionary history of Earth's biodiversity is punctuated by speciation events, often triggered by factors such as changes in climate, the formation of physical barriers like mountains or rivers, or the colonization of new habitats.

Adaptive strategies also play a significant role in enabling organisms to survive and thrive in various environments. An adaptive strategy refers to the suite of physical, behavioural, and physiological traits that improve an organism's chances of survival and reproduction in its specific habitat. These strategies are shaped by the pressures of the environment and can vary widely between species and even within species. For instance, some plants have developed deep root systems to access water in arid regions, while others have evolved mechanisms to store water in their tissues. Animals, too, exhibit a wide range of adaptive strategies, from the migration patterns of birds to the camouflage abilities of insects.

In the Arctic, polar bears have developed several adaptive strategies to survive in extreme cold. Their thick fur and fat layers provide insulation against frigid temperatures, while their keen sense of smell helps them locate prey across vast ice expanses. Similarly, in tropical rainforests, certain frogs have evolved adhesive pads on their feet, allowing them to climb and navigate the dense vegetation easily. These examples underscore the importance of adaptive strategies in helping organisms exploit available resources and withstand environmental pressures.

Genetic variations within populations are essential for fostering evolutionary potential. Genetic variation arises from mutations, gene flow, and sexual reproduction, which introduce new alleles into a population. This genetic diversity provides the raw material upon which natural selection acts. Populations with higher genetic variability are better equipped to adapt to changing conditions, increasing their likelihood of survival over long periods of time.

One striking example of the importance of genetic variation can be seen in the cheetah population. The cheetah has faced several bottlenecks in its evolutionary history, leading to reduced genetic diversity. This lack of genetic variation makes cheetahs more susceptible to diseases and environmental changes, threatening their long-term survival. Conversely, high genetic variability in other species, such as the peppered moth, has allowed rapid adaptation to environmental changes. During the Industrial Revolution, pollution darkened tree trunks, giving dark-colored moths a survival advantage over lighter ones. This shift in allele frequency within the population illustrates how genetic variation can drive rapid evolutionary responses.

The interplay of these evolutionary processes—natural selection, speciation, adaptive strategies, and genetic variation—creates the rich and complex web of life we observe today. Understanding these processes not only illuminates the origins of biodiversity but also underscores the dynamic nature of life on Earth. It highlights the resilience and adaptability of species in the face of challenges, as well as the delicate balance that sustains ecosystems.

As we delve deeper into the complexity of biodiversity, it becomes evident that preserving genetic diversity within populations is crucial for maintaining the evolutionary potential of species. Conservation efforts must prioritise protecting diverse habitats and fostering conditions that allow natural selection and adaptive strategies to continue shaping life forms. By safeguarding the evolutionary processes that generate and sustain biodiversity, we can ensure that future generations inherit a world brimming with the wonder and beauty of life's diversity.

Threats to Biodiversity

Habitat destruction represents one of the most significant threats to biodiversity across the globe. As human populations expand, the demand for land for agriculture, urban development, and infrastructure increases correspondingly. Forests are cleared, wetlands drained, and grasslands converted into farm fields. This widespread alteration of habitats directly leads to the loss of species that rely on these environments. Many organisms have specialised needs and can only thrive in specific conditions found within their native habitats. When these areas are destroyed or fragmented, the plants, animals, and microorganisms that inhabit them often struggle to survive. Moreover, habitat destruction can lead to a decrease in genetic diversity within populations, which is crucial for adaptation and resilience against diseases and changing environmental conditions.

Climate change poses another prominent threat to biodiversity by altering ecosystems worldwide.

Dr. Anthonysamy David

Increasing temperatures, shifting precipitation patterns, and more frequent extreme weather events disrupt the delicate balance of ecosystems. Species adapted to particular climate conditions may find it increasingly difficult to survive as their habitats become unhospitable. For instance, polar bears depend on sea ice for hunting seals, and as global warming causes ice to melt earlier in the season and form later, their ability to find food diminishes. Similarly, coral reefs, which are biodiversity hotspots, are highly sensitive to changes in water temperature. Coral bleaching events, exacerbated by rising sea temperatures, result in the loss of symbiotic algae essential for the survival of corals, leading to extensive reef degradation. Climate change also has indirect effects, such as altering migration patterns, disrupting breeding seasons, and increasing susceptibility to diseases among various species.

Pollution introduces harmful substances into ecosystems, posing a severe threat to biodiversity. Industrial waste, agricultural runoff, and plastic debris are common pollutants that negatively impact flora and fauna. Chemical pollutants such as pesticides, heavy metals, and endocrine disruptors can accumulate in the tissues of living organisms, causing physiological and reproductive harm. For example, agricultural runoff containing nitrogen and phosphorus can lead to nutrient overload in water bodies, causing harmful algal blooms and creating dead zones with low oxygen levels that are inhospitable to aquatic life. Plastic pollution is another growing concern, especially in marine environments. Marine animals often ingest plastic debris, mistaking it for food, which can lead to internal injuries, malnutrition, and death. Additionally, microplastics—tiny plastic particles resulting from the breakdown of larger pieces—can infiltrate the food chain, ultimately affecting a wide range of organisms, including humans.

Understanding Invasive Species

Invasive species are a significant problem for ecosystems around the world. These are plants, animals, or microorganisms that come from other places and are introduced into new environments. When they arrive in a new habitat, they often do not have the natural predators that keep their populations in check. This means they can grow and reproduce without limitation, outcompeting local species for essential resources like food, water, and space.

The Impact on Native Species

When invasive species take hold in an ecosystem, they can cause serious harm to the native species. Native species are those that originally belonged to a specific area, and they have adapted over time to their environment. In contrast, invasive species can disrupt the delicate balance of nature. For example, the brown tree snake, introduced to Guam, has significantly impacted the local bird population. Many native birds on the island have declined or even gone extinct due to the snake's predation.

The presence of the brown tree snake has not just affected the birds directly. Bird species play important roles in an ecosystem, such as seed dispersal and forest regeneration. The loss of these birds can lead to a decline in plant diversity as seeds are no longer spread throughout the area. Without a variety of plants, the forest may suffer, and the overall health of the ecosystem can decline.

The Threat of Invasive Plants

Invasive plants also pose a major threat to native ecosystems. When these plants are introduced, they can grow quickly and take over areas that native species once occupied. For instance, species such as kudzu can form dense mats that block sunlight from reaching the plants underneath. This results in a situation where native plants struggle to survive because they cannot get the light, water, or nutrients they need.

Dense plant growth created by invasive species can reduce habitat availability for other species as well. Native animals that rely on specific plants for food or shelter may find it challenging to survive when their habitat changes drastically. The competition for resources can lead to a decline in local biodiversity, making ecosystems less resilient to environmental changes.

Introduction of New Diseases

Another way that invasive species threaten biodiversity is through disease. Invasive species can bring with them pathogens that native species have never encountered. Since these local species have not developed immunity to these new diseases, they can suffer high mortality rates. For instance, the spread of certain pathogens introduced by invasive species can devastate populations of native plants and animals.

When native populations decline due to disease, the effects ripple through the ecosystem. Fewer native species can lead to reduced genetic diversity, which is crucial for the health and survival of populations over the long term. This, in turn, impacts the entire ecosystem, leading to a less stable environment.

Prevention and Management Strategies

Preventing invasive species from entering new ecosystems is essential. One effective strategy is to educate people about the dangers of releasing pets into the wild or planting non-native species in gardens. By being informed, individuals can make better choices that do not harm local ecosystems. For example, choosing native plants for landscaping can support local wildlife and reduce the risk of introducing invasive species.

Government regulations also play a crucial role in managing invasive species. Laws can be implemented to control the importation of potentially harmful species. Additionally, monitoring programmes can help identify and respond to new invasions quickly. By having a strategy in place for rapid response, it is easier to manage and control invasive populations before they cause significant damage.

Restoration Efforts

In cases where invasive species have already established themselves, restoration efforts can be pursued. Removing invasive species is labor-intensive but necessary. People can participate in local efforts to remove invasive plants, such as pulling them out or applying herbicides. Once the invasive species are managed, planting native species can help restore the ecosystem. These native plants can provide food and shelter for wildlife and promote the recovery of local habitats.

Community involvement can be a powerful tool in fighting against invasive species. Local organisations may offer programmes that educate people about the impact of invasive species and how to help. Individuals can join these programmes to learn more and take active steps in protecting their local ecosystems.

Working Together to Protect Biodiversity

Protecting biodiversity is essential not only for the plants and animals within an ecosystem but also for humans. A healthy ecosystem provides services that benefit people, such as clean air, water, and food resources. By working together to understand the threats invasive species pose, communities can assist in preserving their local environments.

Public awareness campaigns can effectively convey the importance of protecting native species. By promoting native plants and animals, individuals can help raise awareness and encourage others to get involved. When people understand the connection between healthy ecosystems and their own well-being, they are more likely to take action.

Maintaining biodiversity requires a collaborative effort from everyone. Whether through individual actions, community programmes, or government initiatives, every effort counts. Even simple actions, like cleaning hiking boots before visiting new areas or not introducing non-native species, can make a difference in protecting local ecosystems.

In summary, invasive species present a substantial threat to biodiversity and ecosystem health. By understanding their impact, taking preventive measures, and actively participating in restoration efforts, we can work towards a more balanced and healthy environment for all species to thrive.

Addressing these major threats requires comprehensive and coordinated conservation efforts. Protecting existing habitats through the establishment of protected areas, enforcing regulations to curb pollution, implementing sustainable agricultural practices, and controlling the introduction and spread of invasive species are essential strategies. Additionally, promoting climate resilience through the restoration of degraded ecosystems and the adoption of climate-smart conservation practices will help buffer biodiversity against the impacts of climate change. Engaging local communities and stakeholders in conservation initiatives fosters a collaborative approach, ensuring that efforts are sustainable and culturally appropriate.

Conservation Efforts

Advocating for biodiversity protection is essential to maintaining the balance of ecosystems and ensuring a sustainable future. One of the most effective ways to protect biodiversity is by establishing protected areas that preserve critical habitats. These designated regions can shelter diverse species, allowing them to thrive without interference from human activities. However, while the creation of protected areas plays a significant role in conservation, it is not sufficient on its own.

Protected areas must be managed effectively to meet their goal of preserving biodiversity. Many existing protected areas suffer from inadequate resources and enforcement, limiting their effectiveness (UNESCO, 2024). To address this, there is a need for enhanced management practices, better funding, and stronger legal frameworks.

Additionally, with climate change altering habitats, protected area networks may need realignment to ensure they continue to support the species they were intended to protect.

Beyond protected areas, implementing conservation policies at both global and local levels is vital. International conventions such as the Convention on Biological Diversity provide frameworks for countries to cooperate on conservation efforts. At a national level, governments can implement laws and regulations that directly protect species and habitats. Local conservation policies should be tailored to fit the unique needs and challenges of specific regions. Collaborative efforts between countries and within communities can create comprehensive strategies that address biodiversity loss more effectively.

Sustainable development practices are another crucial component of mitigating human impact on biodiversity. Unsustainable practices like deforestation, overfishing, and pollution contribute significantly to habitat destruction and species extinction. Transitioning to sustainable methods involves using resources efficiently, reducing waste, and minimising environmental footprints. For example, sustainable agriculture practices can include crop rotation, reduced pesticide use, and conservation tillage. In forestry, techniques such as selective logging and reforestation help maintain forest health and biodiversity.

Public awareness and education also play a critical role in promoting biodiversity conservation. Raising awareness about the importance of biodiversity and the threats it faces can inspire individuals and communities to take action. Educational programmes can teach people how their daily choices impact the environment and what they can do to contribute to conservation efforts. Schools, media campaigns, and community initiatives can all be powerful tools for increasing public engagement in biodiversity protection.

Research has shown that higher levels of public awareness correlate with positive attitudes towards biodiversity conservation (Ibrahim et al., 2022). This underscores the importance of incorporating biodiversity education into broader educational curricula and public outreach campaigns. By fostering a greater understanding of biodiversity among the general population, we can cultivate a culture that values and actively participates in conservation.

Addressing biodiversity loss requires a multifaceted approach that includes establishing protected areas, implementing effective conservation policies, adopting sustainable development practices, and enhancing public awareness and education. Each of these components is interrelated and reinforces the others, creating a robust framework for protecting biodiversity.

The Human Impact

The relationship between humans and biodiversity is complex and multifaceted. Human activities, such as deforestation, pollution, urbanisation, and climate change, have significant impacts on biodiversity. At the same time, humans can play a crucial role in conservation efforts to preserve biodiversity through various means.

Human activities contribute significantly to biodiversity loss, primarily through deforestation, pollution, and urbanisation. Deforestation, particularly in tropical rainforests, leads to habitat destruction, which displaces species and reduces available habitats and food sources. As trees are cleared for agriculture, mining, and urban development, the natural landscapes that support diverse ecosystems are diminished (The Royal Society, 2024). Pollution also poses a major threat to biodiversity. Chemical substances from industrial runoff, agricultural pesticides, and fertilisers contaminate soil and water bodies, leading to detrimental effects on plant and animal life. Additionally, noise and light pollution can disrupt the behaviour and reproductive patterns of various species. Urbanisation further exacerbates these issues as cities expand into natural habitats, causing fragmentation and degradation of ecosystems.

Moreover, human-induced climate change has emerged as a critical driver of biodiversity decline. The burning of fossil fuels and extensive agricultural practices release large amounts of greenhouse gases, such as carbon dioxide and methane, into the atmosphere. These gases trap heat, causing global temperatures to rise and climate patterns to shift. As a result, species are forced to adapt, migrate, or face extinction due to changing environmental conditions, such as altered rainfall patterns and rising sea levels (Khan Academy, n.d.).

Despite these challenges, humans have the capacity to mitigate biodiversity loss through concerted conservation efforts. Conservation involves protecting species and their habitats, and it encompasses various strategies and practices. One critical approach is establishing protected areas, such as national parks and wildlife reserves, which safeguard essential habitats and provide refuge for endangered species. Additionally, the implementation of international and local legislation can help curtail activities that threaten biodiversity. For example, laws that regulate hunting, fishing, and deforestation can reduce overexploitation and habitat destruction.

Furthermore, captive breeding programmes play a vital role in conservation by maintaining healthy populations of endangered species. These programmes facilitate the reproduction and genetic diversity of species in captivity, which can eventually be reintroduced into the wild. Another significant conservation measure is habitat restoration, which involves rehabilitating degraded ecosystems to restore their ecological functions and support biodiversity. Restoration projects may include reforestation, wetland rehabilitation, and soil stabilisation efforts.

Understanding ecological interdependence is crucial for effective biodiversity conservation. Ecosystems are intricate networks of organisms that rely on one another for survival. The removal or decline of one species can have cascading effects on the entire ecosystem. For example, the extinction of a predator can lead to an overpopulation of its prey, resulting in imbalances that affect vegetation and other species. Thus, preserving biodiversity requires a holistic understanding of these interconnections and the roles different species play within their ecosystems.

Promoting sustainable living practices is another key aspect of mitigating negative impacts on biodiversity. Sustainable practices aim to balance human needs with environmental preservation, reducing the exploitation of natural resources and minimising ecological footprints. One such practice is responsible consumption, which involves making informed choices about the products we use and their environmental impact. This includes supporting eco-friendly products, reducing waste through recycling and reuse, and opting for sustainably sourced materials.

Additionally, sustainable agriculture can significantly reduce biodiversity loss. Practices such as crop rotation, organic farming, and agroforestry promote soil health, reduce chemical inputs, and create habitats for beneficial species. Agroforestry, for instance, integrates trees and shrubs into agricultural landscapes, providing habitat corridors for wildlife and enhancing biodiversity. Sustainable fisheries management is another important area, focussing on regulating fishing practices to prevent overfishing and protect marine ecosystems.

Urban planning and development also play a crucial role in preserving biodiversity. Incorporating green spaces, such as parks and urban forests, within cities can provide habitats for various species and improve the quality of life for residents. Green infrastructure, such as green roofs and walls, can mitigate the urban heat island effect, reduce energy consumption, and support urban biodiversity.

Public awareness and education are essential components of biodiversity conservation. Educating communities about the importance of biodiversity and the threats it faces can inspire collective action and foster a sense of responsibility towards the environment. Environmental education programmes can be integrated into school curricula, community workshops, and public campaigns to raise awareness and promote sustainable behaviours.

Dr. Anthonysamy David

Bringing It All Together

This chapter has delved into the multifaceted aspects of biodiversity, highlighting its significance for ecosystem stability and human well-being. We have examined how diverse ecosystems are better equipped to withstand environmental stresses and the critical roles various species play within their habitats. The chapter also addressed the tangible and intangible benefits of biodiversity, from ecosystem services like food and clean water to cultural enrichment and mental well-being. Furthermore, it emphasised the urgent need for conservation efforts to mitigate the severe consequences of biodiversity loss driven by human activities such as deforestation, pollution, and climate change.

We also explored the effectiveness of different conservation strategies, including the establishment of protected areas, sustainable development practices, and international cooperation. It is clear that preserving biodiversity requires a multi-faceted approach involving local communities, governments, scientists, and global organisations. By understanding the unique contributions of various ecosystems and fostering collaborative conservation initiatives, we can enhance the resilience of our natural world. This comprehensive approach not only safeguards the intricate balance of nature but also ensures the continued provision of essential ecosystem services upon which human societies depend.

Reference List

Biodiversity: Understanding its Significance and Conservation Nature and Culture International . (2024, January 27). Nature and Culture International: Bringing People Together to Save Wild Places. https://www.natureandculture.org/biodiversity-understanding-its-significance-and-conservation/

Centre for Biological Diversity. (2019). *The Elements of Biodiversity* . Biologicaldiversity.org. https://www.biologicaldiversity.org/programs/biodiversity/elements_of_biodiversity/

Ibrahim, M. S. N., Assim, M. I. S. A., Johari, S., Mohammad, S. K. W., Afandi, S. H. M., & Hassan, S. (2022, December 28). *Public awareness on biodiversity conservation and well-being: case of Gunung Mulu National Park, Sarawak* . GeoJournal. https://doi.org/10.1007/s10708-022-10818-x

Khan Academy . (n.d.). *Human impact on ecosystems review (article)* . Khan Academy. https://www.khanacademy.org/science/ap-biology/ecology-ap/disruptions-to-ecosystems/a/hs-human-impact-on-ecosystems-review

The Royal Society. (2024). *What is the human impact on biodiversity? | Royal Society* . Royalsociety.org. https://royalsociety.org/news-resources/projects/biodiversity/human-impact-on-biodiversity/

UNESCO. (2024, February 5). *Conservation and sustainable use of biodiversity | UNESCO* . Www.unesco.org. https://www.unesco.org/en/biodiversity/conservation

Chapter 10

The Hidden Life of Trees: What They Feel, How They Communicate

Tree communication reveals a fascinating world where trees interact with each other through an underground network. Known as the 'Wood Wide Web,' this network consists of mycorrhizal fungi connecting tree roots, allowing not only resource sharing but also sophisticated forms of communication. The subterranean web facilitates nutrient and water distribution among trees, supporting mutual growth and survival within forest ecosystems. This intricate connection helps older trees nourish younger saplings, ensuring even those in shaded areas receive essential nutrients.

In this chapter, we will delve into the mechanisms by which trees communicate through this vast fungal network, exploring both the benefits and complexities of these interactions. We will examine how trees transmit chemical signals to respond to environmental threats, thereby showcasing their adaptive behaviours. Furthermore, the chapter will highlight scientific research on the preferential sharing of resources among related trees and the broader ecological significance of these networks. The exploration will provide insights into the symbiotic relationships that sustain forest health and resilience, emphasising the need for further study and conservation of these sophisticated natural systems.

Tree Communication

Understanding how trees communicate through an underground network is key to appreciating the intricate relationships within forest ecosystems. Trees use what is known as the 'Wood Wide Web,' a term coined to describe an extensive network of mycorrhizal fungi connecting tree roots. This subterranean web enables trees not only to link their root systems but also to facilitate the sharing of resources like nutrients and water.

The mycorrhizal network consists primarily of fungal filaments called hyphae, which intertwine with tree roots. These hyphae create a vast underground network that allows trees to engage in mutual support. For instance, older trees can share their surplus nutrients with younger saplings through this network. These saplings rely on the nutrients provided by more mature trees because they frequently grow in shaded areas where there is insufficient sunlight for photosynthesis (Holewinski, 2019).

This nutrient exchange plays a crucial role in maintaining the overall health of the forest. Trees absorb necessary minerals from the soil, including phosphorus and nitrogen, which are then distributed through the mycorrhizal network to other trees. This process ensures that even the weaker or younger members of the ecosystem receive the sustenance they need to thrive. Additionally, mycorrhizal fungi benefit from this relationship by absorbing carbohydrates produced by tree photosynthesis, thus sustaining their own growth (Pappas, 2023).

Beyond nutrient sharing, the mycorrhizal network also serves as a communication channel. Trees can transmit chemical signals through these fungal pathways, enabling them to respond to various threats. When a tree experiences environmental stress, such as an insect infestation, it releases distress signals into the network. Neighbouring trees receiving these signals can then activate their defence mechanisms. For example, if one tree detects an insect threat, it might increase the production of protective chemicals to ward off the invaders. Through the network, nearby trees can also start producing similar defensive compounds, thus preparing in advance for potential attacks (Holewinski, 2019).

The idea of trees sending distress signals challenges traditional views of plant behaviour, highlighting a level of complexity previously attributed mainly to animals. This adaptive capacity allows trees to react promptly to changes in their environment, enhancing their chances of survival. The mycorrhizal network's ability to facilitate communication highlights the interdependence within forest communities. Older, well-established trees, often referred to as "mother trees," play a vital role in detecting and responding to the needs of the surrounding community. They are crucial nodes within the network, offering stability by maintaining a consistent supply of nutrients and water to younger trees (Holewinski, 2019).

Scientific research supports the notion that trees can recognise the root tips of their relatives and preferentially direct resources towards them. Studies involving Douglas-fir trees indicate that these trees show favouritism when distributing carbon and nutrients through the fungal network, prioritising their kin over non-relatives (Holewinski, 2019). This discovery suggests a sophisticated level of interaction where trees are not solely competing for resources but are also engaging in selective assistance, thereby promoting the wellbeing of genetically related individuals.

While some scientists remain sceptical about the extent of tree cooperation, the evidence supporting the existence and functionality of the mycorrhizal network is compelling. Mycorrhizal networks offer practical ecological benefits, such as enhancing soil structure, retaining moisture, and reducing erosion. These benefits, in turn, contribute to the resilience and sustainability of forest ecosystems.

Nevertheless, it is essential to approach these findings with a balanced perspective. While the concept of the 'Wood Wide Web' has gained popularity, further research is necessary to fully understand its complexities and variations across different forest types. Challenges such as the ephemeral nature of fungal networks and the difficulties in studying them in natural settings complicate the research efforts. Some studies have pointed out that while mycorrhizal networks exist, the evidence for their role in facilitating widespread cooperation among trees remains inconclusive (Pappas, 2023).

Dr. Anthonysamy David

Tree Behaviour and Social Life

The social behaviours of trees reveal a complex network of interactions that are not just fascinating but vital for the ecological stability of forests. Trees exhibit social behaviours akin to those of animals, communicating with one another about threats and sharing resources to ensure the survival of their community.

Trees use various methods to communicate. One primary mode of communication is through chemical, hormonal, and slow-pulsing electrical signals. These signals can transmit distress calls about insect attacks, droughts, or diseases to neighbouring trees. For example, when a giraffe nibbles on the leaves of an acacia tree, the injured tree releases ethylene gas, which warns nearby trees to produce tannins in their leaves as a defence mechanism (Grant, 2018).

In addition to aerial communication, trees also rely on subterranean networks. Known as the "Wood Wide Web," these underground systems consist of mycorrhizal fungi that connect the roots of different trees. Through these networks, trees can share essential nutrients like water and minerals. This fungal network allows older trees, or "mother trees," to support their offspring by providing them with the necessary resources. Researchers have found that mature trees will often pump sugars into the roots of saplings that do not receive enough sunlight to photosynthesize efficiently, thus ensuring their growth and survival (Jabr, 2020).

For the younger members of the forest, the interdependence that these networks facilitate is essential. Without the assistance of older trees, many young trees would struggle to survive in shaded conditions. The provision of resources is not limited to just parent-offspring relationships; it extends to other members of the forest community as well. For instance, researchers have discovered that even decomposing stumps can remain alive for centuries, nourished by surrounding trees through the fungal network (Grant, 2018).

This collective behaviour among trees challenges the traditional view that trees are solitary competitors vying for resources. Instead, forests act as a unified entity where the strong support the weak, thereby enhancing the resilience of the ecosystem. Scientists have observed that trees of the same species and even different species form alliances, sharing resources to stabilise the forest environment. For example, studies have shown that removing certain tree species from a forest can lead to increased vulnerability to disease and environmental stressors for the remaining trees, emphasising the importance of biodiversity and cooperation (Grant, 2018).

Moreover, these social behaviours extend beyond nutrient sharing. Trees adjust their growth patterns based on those of their neighbours. They avoid encroaching on each other's space to maximise sunlight exposure and maintain balance within the ecosystem. Researchers have noted that trees growing close together tend to synchronise their growth cycles, ensuring mutual benefit. This phenomenon is evident in the way trees allocate resources during seasonal changes, effectively managing the collective distribution of nutrients and water.

However, these intricate relationships are not without conflict. Some scientists argue that what appears as cooperative behaviour might sometimes be reciprocal exploitation. Fungi, essential for nutrient exchange, can also control the flow of resources, favouring certain trees over others based on their own benefits. Studies have shown that fungi may withhold nutrients from plants that do not provide sufficient carbon, creating a dynamic of negotiation and tradeoffs within the network (Jabr, 2020).

Regardless of the underlying dynamics, the result of these interactions is a more resilient forest ecosystem. The social life of trees underscores the importance of maintaining old-growth forests and their diverse communities. Disturbances such as deforestation and climate change threaten these delicate networks, making conservation efforts crucial. Understanding the social behaviours of trees can inform better forest management practices, aiming to preserve the intricate and beneficial relationships that sustain forest ecosystems.

For instance, effective conservation strategies could involve protecting mother trees that play a pivotal role in nurturing young saplings. Ensuring that these keystone trees remain intact can help maintain the essential nutrient and water exchanges necessary for the forest's overall health. Additionally, promoting mixed-species forests rather than monocultures could enhance resilience against pests and diseases, further supported by the cooperative interactions among different tree species.

The insights gained from studying the social behaviours of trees offer valuable lessons for human societies as well. Just as trees thrive through cooperation and resource sharing, human communities can benefit from embracing principles of mutual support and collaboration. By recognising the interconnectedness of natural systems, we can adopt more sustainable practices that align with the inherent wisdom found in forest ecosystems.

Trees as Communal Organisms

Understanding tree communities and their mutualistic relationships is crucial for comprehending the intricate dynamics that sustain forest ecosystems. Trees do not exist in isolation; rather, they form interconnected communities that engage in mutualistic relationships, sharing resources and support.

One of the most significant aspects of these relationships is the exchange of nutrients. In a well-functioning forest ecosystem, trees have developed mechanisms to share nutrients with weaker or younger trees. This process often occurs through a network of mycorrhizal fungi, which connect the roots of different trees, enabling the transfer of essential nutrients such as nitrogen, phosphorus, and water. The "Wood Wide Web" facilitates this nutrient exchange, ensuring that even the weakest members of the community have access to what they need to grow and thrive (Aerts & Honnay, 2011).

This nutrient-sharing behaviour is not just an act of altruism but a strategic move for the overall health of the forest. By supporting the growth of weaker or younger trees, the older and more established trees help maintain the structural integrity and diversity of the forest. This, in turn, enhances the forest's resilience against environmental stresses such as droughts and diseases. When all the trees in a community are healthy, the entire ecosystem stands a better chance of surviving adverse conditions (Grossiord, 2020).

Furthermore, trees engage in reciprocal relationships with various organisms in their environment. For instance, trees provide shelter and food for animals such as birds, insects, and mammals. In return, these animals contribute to the dispersal of seeds, pollination, and pest control, creating a balanced and self-sustaining ecosystem. Birds play a particularly important role in seed dispersal, helping to spread tree species across different areas, thereby promoting biodiversity and forest regeneration (Aerts & Honnay, 2011).

Moreover, the cooperation among trees and other organisms extends below the ground. Soil microbial communities, including bacteria and fungi, interact with tree roots, facilitating nutrient uptake and enhancing soil fertility. Arbuscular mycorrhizal fungi (AMF) and ectomycorrhizal fungi (ECMF) are particularly significant in this context. AMF primarily provide trees with access to soil phosphorus, while ECMF can mobilise both organic and mineral resources, contributing to the overall nutrient cycle within the forest (Sachsenmaier et al., 2024).

The mutualistic relationships within tree communities also play a vital role in sustaining biodiversity and ecosystem stability. Biodiversity is essential for the resilience of forest ecosystems, as it ensures that various species can perform different ecological roles. For example, different tree species may have varying abilities to withstand drought, disease, or other stressors. When a diverse array of species coexists, the likelihood increases that some will survive and maintain ecosystem functions even under adverse conditions. This diversity acts as a buffer, protecting the forest from catastrophic events and contributing to its long-term stability (Grossiord et al., 2014).

Additionally, the interdependence among trees fosters an environment where positive feedback loops enhance ecosystem resilience. For instance, trees that are well-nourished due to mutualistic nutrient sharing produce more robust root systems and leaf canopies. These, in turn, contribute to soil stabilisation, water retention, and the overall microclimate of the forest. As a result, the forest becomes more resilient to extreme weather events such as heavy rainfall or prolonged drought periods (Schnabel et al., 2021).

Another critical aspect of tree communities is their contribution to carbon sequestration. Forests act as significant carbon sinks, absorbing and storing carbon dioxide from the atmosphere. This function is vital for mitigating climate change. The cooperative interactions within tree communities enhance their capacity for carbon storage by maintaining healthy and diverse forest structures. Trees with strong mutualistic relationships are more likely to thrive, grow larger, and store more carbon over their lifetimes (Cardinale et al., 2013).

Tree Sensitivity and Adaptation

In the fascinating world of trees, understanding their sensory capabilities and adaptive behaviours uncovers a complex and dynamic natural system. Trees exhibit an extraordinary ability to perceive changes in their environment through various means, including light, gravity, and physical damage. This perception is crucial for their survival and optimal function within their ecosystems.

Trees perceive changes in light through specialised photoreceptors. These receptors allow them to detect different wavelengths of light, enabling processes such as phototropism—where plants grow towards light. By growing towards light, trees maximise their photosynthetic potential, ensuring they capture sufficient energy for growth and development. This adaptive behaviour is critical in forest environments where competition for sunlight is intense. For instance, in dense forests, tree seedlings must quickly adapt to shaded conditions by elongating their stems towards gaps or openings in the canopy that let light through. This response helps them reach areas with better light availability, thus enhancing their survival chances (OpenStaxCollege, 2012).

Additionally, trees can sense gravity through gravitropism, which plays a pivotal role in their orientation and structural integrity. The roots grow downward, anchoring the tree securely in the soil and allowing efficient water and nutrient uptake. Conversely, the shoots grow upward, facilitating access to light and air. This dual response ensures trees maintain stability and proper orientation regardless of uneven terrain or other external influences. Auxins, a group of plant hormones that redistribute within plant tissues to signal growth direction, mediate gravitropic responses. Understanding these mechanisms gives insight into how trees adapt to their physical surroundings and even recover from disturbances like storms or heavy winds.

Physical damage, such as wounds from herbivores or mechanical injuries, also triggers sensory responses in trees. When damaged, trees initiate a series of chemical and physiological reactions to seal wounds and defend against further harm. Compounds like tannins and resins are produced to deter pests and pathogens. Additionally, some trees release volatile organic compounds to signal nearby plants about the threat, prompting a collective defence response. This sophisticated communication system underscores the intricate ways trees manage and mitigate environmental stressors, ensuring their longevity and resilience in diverse habitats.

Trees' ability to adjust growth patterns in response to varying environmental conditions demonstrates their remarkable adaptability. For example, they can optimise leaf orientation and branching patterns to maximise sunlight exposure in low-light conditions. In higher-altitude regions, trees often develop shorter and sturdier forms to withstand wind pressure and snow loads. Adaptations like these ensure trees not only survive but thrive in their specific ecological niches. Their ability to fine-tune growth based on local conditions highlights the interplay between genetic predisposition and environmental stimuli.

Sensory perception also aids trees in managing water and nutrient uptake effectively. Root systems explore the soil, detecting moisture gradients and nutrient concentrations and allowing trees to adjust root growth accordingly. During dry periods, roots may grow deeper to access groundwater reserves. In nutrient-poor soils, symbiotic relationships with mycorrhizal fungi enhance nutrient absorption, especially phosphorus. These adaptive strategies ensure trees maintain their metabolic functions even under suboptimal conditions. Trees equipped with robust sensory mechanisms are more adept at coping with environmental fluctuations, contributing to their success across various ecosystems.

Adaptation is crucial for trees' survival in differing climates and geographical regions. In arid environments, some species have developed deep root systems or thickened leaves to minimise water loss. Others may enter a state of dormancy during extreme weather conditions, conserving resources until favourable conditions return. Such adaptations enable trees to inhabit a wide range of ecosystems, from tropical rainforests to temperate woodlands to boreal forests. Each species' unique set of adaptive traits reflects a long evolutionary history shaped by environmental pressures and interactions.

Moreover, trees play a significant role in maintaining ecological balance and supporting biodiversity. As primary producers, they form the foundation of terrestrial food webs, providing habitat and resources for a myriad of organisms. Their ability to adapt and thrive underpins the health and stability of ecosystems. For instance, in a forest setting, the diversity of tree species and their various adaptive strategies create a mosaic of microhabitats, supporting diverse plant and animal communities. By understanding trees' sensory and adaptive mechanisms, researchers can better appreciate the complexities of forest dynamics and the importance of conserving these vital ecosystems.

Human Impact on Forests

In recent decades, human activities have significantly impacted tree networks and ecosystems. Among the most detrimental activities are deforestation and climate change. These actions disrupt the delicate balance of tree networks, posing profound threats not only to individual trees but also to broader ecological systems.

Large-scale tree removal results from deforestation, which is a result of logging, urban development, and agricultural expansion. This disruption is catastrophic for tree networks, which rely on interconnected root systems and mycorrhizal fungi to share nutrients and resources. When sections of a forest are cleared, these intricate networks are severed, reducing the ability of the remaining trees to communicate and support each other. Furthermore, deforestation results in habitat loss, leading to the decline of numerous plant and animal species that depend on forested environments.

Climate change exacerbates these problems by altering weather patterns, increasing the frequency of extreme weather events, and shifting temperature ranges. Trees are particularly sensitive to such changes; they thrive within specific climatic conditions that have evolved over centuries. For instance, prolonged droughts can weaken trees, making them more susceptible to diseases and pests. Similarly, unseasonably warm winters may prevent trees from entering the necessary periods of dormancy, impairing their growth cycles. The collective impact of these disruptions can lead to reduced forest resilience and biodiversity.

The broader ecological implications of these threats are profound. Forests play a critical role in regulating the Earth's climate by sequestering carbon dioxide, a major greenhouse gas. Healthy forests absorb significant amounts of carbon, mitigating the effects of climate change. However, when trees are cut down or weakened by changing climates, this capability diminishes. Additionally, soil erosion can increase in deforested areas, leading to the loss of fertile land and further contributing to environmental degradation.

To address these challenges, effective forest management and conservation efforts are paramount. Forest management practices must prioritise the preservation and restoration of tree networks. One such approach is the establishment of protected areas where logging and land conversion are restricted, allowing ecosystems to recover. Reforestation and afforestation initiatives can also help restore degraded lands and create new tree networks. Implementing sustainable logging practices, such as selective logging and maintaining buffer zones around waterways, can mitigate the impact on existing forests.

Conservation efforts should focus on preserving old-growth forests, which often harbour the most complex and resilient tree networks. These ancient trees serve as keystones in their ecosystems, providing stability and supporting diverse biological communities. Protecting these invaluable resources requires stringent policies and enforcement against illegal logging and land encroachment.

Understanding the communication mechanisms within tree networks is crucial for developing sustainable forestry practices. Trees communicate through intricate signalling processes involving chemical, electrical, and hormonal messages. By recognising how trees respond to stressors like pests or environmental changes, we can implement strategies to bolster forest health. For example, research has shown that trees emit distress signals through their root systems and foliage when under attack by herbivores or pathogens. Neighbouring trees can sense these signals and activate their own defence mechanisms, creating a collective resistance against threats.

Incorporating knowledge of tree communication into forest management can enhance reforestation efforts. Selecting tree species that effectively communicate and support each other can foster robust ecosystems. Additionally, planting a mix of tree species can recreate the diversity found in natural forests, promoting resilience against diseases and environmental changes.

Effective forest management involves continuous monitoring and adaptive strategies. Utilising technology, such as remote sensing and drones, can provide valuable data on forest health, allowing for timely interventions. Community involvement is also essential; engaging local populations in conservation efforts ensures that initiatives are culturally appropriate and sustainable. Educating communities about the importance of tree networks and ecosystems fosters a sense of stewardship and encourages participation in reforestation projects.

Moreover, international cooperation is vital in addressing the global issue of deforestation and climate change. Collaborative efforts can lead to the exchange of best practices and resources, enhancing the effectiveness of conservation measures. Programmes that provide financial incentives for reducing deforestation, such as REDD+ (Reducing Emissions from Deforestation and Forest Degradation), can motivate countries to prioritise forest conservation.

Throughout these endeavours, it is imperative to recognise the intrinsic value of forests beyond their ecological roles. Forests hold cultural, spiritual, and economic significance for many communities worldwide. Integrating traditional knowledge and practices with modern scientific approaches can yield innovative solutions for forest management.

Concluding Thoughts

This chapter has delved into the intricate interactions and communication mechanisms within tree ecosystems, emphasising their ecological significance. We have explored how trees use the mycorrhizal network, often referred to as the "Wood Wide Web," to share essential nutrients and water, maintaining overall forest health. Through this underground network, trees can alert nearby trees to environmental stressors, triggering their defense mechanisms. These findings challenge traditional views of plant behaviour and highlight the interconnectedness and interdependence within forest ecosystems.

The evidence supporting mycorrhizal networks suggests practical ecological benefits such as enhancing soil structure and resilience against environmental stresses. However, it is crucial to approach these discoveries with a balanced perspective, recognising the need for further research to fully understand the complexities of tree cooperation and communication. By continuing to investigate these interactions, we can better appreciate the sophisticated dynamics that sustain forest ecosystems and inform sustainable forestry practices, ultimately contributing to conservation efforts and ecological stability.

Reference List

Aerts, R., & Honnay, O. (2011). *Forest restoration, biodiversity and ecosystem functioning* . BMC Ecology. https://doi.org/10.1186/1472-6785-11-29

Braga, C. (2021). *Effects of Deforestation on Humans and the Environment* . The Humane League. https://thehumaneleague.org/article/effects-of-deforestation

Filipenco, D. (2022, May 17). . DevelopmentAid. https://www.developmentaid.org/news-stream/post/143191/the-effects-of-deforestation-on-humans-the-environment-and-biodiversity

Georgia Tech Biological Sciences. (n.d.). *Plant Hormones and Sensory Systems Organismal Biology* . Organismalbio.biosci.gatech.edu. https://organismalbio.biosci.gatech.edu/chemical-and-electrical-signals/plant-hormones-and-sensory-systems/

Grant, R. (2018, March). *Do Trees Talk to Each Other?* Smithsonian; Smithsonian.com. https://www.smithsonianmag.com/science-nature/the-whispering-trees-180968084/

Holewinski, B. (2019, May 28). *Underground Networking: The Amazing Connections Beneath Your Feet, National Forest Foundation* . Nationalforests.org. https://www.nationalforests.org/blog/underground-mycorrhizal-network

Jabr, F. (2020, December 3). *The Social Life of Forests* . The New York Times. https://www.nytimes.com/interactive/2020/12/02/magazine/tree-communication-mycorrhiza.html

OpenStaxCollege. (2012, August 22). *Plant Sensory Systems and Responses* . Pressbooks-

Dev.oer.hawaii.edu. https://pressbooks-dev.oer.hawaii.edu/biology/chapter/plant-sensory-systems-and-responses/

Pappas, S. (2023, February 13). *Do Trees Really Support Each Other through a Network of Fungi?* Scientific American. https://www.scientificamerican.com/article/do-trees-support-each-other-through-a-network-of-fungi/

Sachsenmaier, L., Schnabel, F., Dietrich, P., Eisenhauer, N., Ferlian, O., Quosh, J., Richter, R., & Wirth, C. (2024, July 12). *Forest growth resistance and resilience to the 2018–2020 drought depend on tree diversity and mycorrhizal type* . Journal of Ecology; Wiley. https://doi.org/10.1111/1365-2745.14360

Chapter11

A World of Insects: A Photographic Tour of Insect Diversity

Insects, the most diverse group of organisms on Earth, showcase an impressive array of forms, colours, and behaviours. The ability to capture these intricate details through advanced photographic techniques is employed in our book, "A World of Insects: A Photographic Tour of Insect Diversity." The book uses high-quality photographs to present a visually rich display of insect life. These images are not only beautiful but also carefully curated to reveal the complexities of insect anatomy and behaviour.

This chapter delves into various aspects of insect diversity using stunning photography and insightful content. Detailed images highlight anatomical structures like wings and exoskeletons, showing their evolutionary adaptations. Readers will explore the vibrant coloration and patterns that insects use for survival. Dynamic photographs capture moments of feeding, mating, and territorial defence, providing glimpses into the active lives of these creatures. Additionally, the book integrates art with scientific observations, making complex biological concepts accessible and engaging. This visual documentation also serves educational purposes, allowing researchers to study insects and educators to engage students effectively.

Visual Presentation: A Feast for the Eyes

Insects, the most diverse group of organisms on Earth, present a fascinating array of forms, colours, and behaviours. Capturing these intricate details requires not only a keen eye but also advanced photographic techniques. Our book, "A World of Insects: A Photographic Tour of Insect Diversity," employs high-quality photographs to highlight the visually rich presentation of insect life. These images are not just beautiful; they are meticulously curated to reveal the hidden complexities that define insect anatomy and behaviour.

One of the standout features of this book is its focus on capturing the detailed anatomical structures of insects. High-resolution photographs allow readers to see the fine details of wings, antennae, and exoskeletons. The delicate venation in an insect's wings or the segmented structure of their antennae provides insights into their evolutionary adaptations. For example, the transparent yet robust nature of dragonfly wings illustrates how these insects have evolved for agile flight. The hardened exoskeletons of beetles, shown in close-up, not only highlight their protective function but also their role in supporting muscle attachment, which is crucial for their movement and survival.

Equally compelling is the book's showcase of the remarkable coloration and patterns found in various insects. These colours and patterns are more than mere aesthetics; they play vital roles in survival and behaviour. Butterflies, for instance, exhibit vibrant colours that can serve as warnings to predators about their toxicity. Similarly, the intricate patterns on moths provide camouflage, blending them with their surroundings to avoid detection. By featuring such vivid imagery, the book underscores how coloration and patterns are integral to the strategies insects use to interact with their environment.

Beyond static representation, the book excels at presenting dynamic images of insect behaviours. Photographs capturing moments of feeding, mating, and territorial defence offer a glimpse into the active lives of these creatures. An image of a praying mantis in mid-strike during a hunt demonstrates its predatory skills and the precision of its movements. Likewise, photographs of bees collecting pollen not only highlight their essential role in pollination but also their complex social behaviours within hives. The mating rituals of fireflies, with their bioluminescent signals, are captured in stunning detail, showcasing the interplay between visual communication and reproductive success.

The combination of artistic photography with scientific observation creates an immersive experience for readers. The artistic aspect draws attention to the beauty and diversity of insects, making the book appealing even to those with a casual interest. At the same time, the scientific observations embedded in the captions and descriptions provide educational value. For instance, while an image might initially attract due to its aesthetic appeal, the accompanying text explaining the ecological role of the featured insect elevates the reader's understanding and appreciation.

This integration of art and science is particularly evident in sections that discuss insect interactions with their habitats. High-quality images of insects in their natural settings highlight the interconnectedness of ecosystems. A photograph of a cicada emerging from its exuviae on a tree trunk not only captures the moment of transformation but also hints at the cyclical nature of life processes in nature. Similarly, pictures of ants herding aphids or termites constructing mounds illustrate the complex social structures and environmental engineering undertaken by these species.

Moreover, the book addresses the importance of such visual documentation for research and education. Detailed images of insects enable researchers to study morphological traits without the need for physical specimens, thereby preserving biodiversity. Educators can use these photographs to engage students, offering a visual gateway to the complexities of entomological studies. The clarity and precision of the images make it easier to explain concepts such as metamorphosis, mimicry, and symbiosis, bridging the gap between textbook learning and real-world observation.

For the readers, this visually rich presentation not only enhances their understanding of insect diversity but also fosters a deeper appreciation for these often-overlooked creatures. It becomes apparent that insects are not merely pests or background noise in our environment; they are sophisticated beings with intricate designs and behaviours that contribute significantly to the world's ecosystems. The book thus serves as both a feast for the eyes and a wellspring of knowledge, encouraging conservation efforts by highlighting the beauty and complexity of insect life.

Diverse Insect Life: A Broad Spectrum of Species

Insect species represent one of the most diverse groups of organisms on the planet, inhabiting nearly every conceivable ecosystem. A comprehensive exploration of insect diversity reveals fascinating aspects of both common and obscure species. This chapter delves into these varied species to highlight the complexity and richness of insect life.

Butterflies and bees are among the most familiar insects, often recognised for their beauty and critical role in pollination. Butterflies, with their vibrant colours and delicate wings, serve as significant pollinators while also acting as indicators of ecological health. Bees, critical for their pollination services, contribute immensely to agricultural productivity and biodiversity. Lesser-known species, such as mantids and dragonflies, showcase equally intriguing characteristics. Mantids, known for their predatory prowess, exhibit a captivating mix of camouflage and agility that allows them to capture prey efficiently. Dragonflies, ancient insects dating back over 300 million years, are renowned for their aerial acrobatics and are key predators of mosquitoes and other small insects.

Exploring insect diversity also involves examining the various habitats they occupy. Insects thrive in a range of environments, from dense forests and sprawling grasslands to intricate wetland ecosystems and bustling urban areas. Each habitat presents unique challenges and opportunities, showcasing the adaptability and resilience of different insect species. Forests provide a rich tapestry of resources where beetles decompose wood, butterflies feed on nectar, and ants create complex colonies. Grasslands, with their open spaces and abundant plant life, support a host of herbivorous insects like locusts and grasshoppers, which play crucial roles in the food web. Wetlands, teeming with moisture and vegetation, are home to diverse species, including water striders and damselflies, adapted to life in aquatic or semi-aquatic settings. Urban areas, despite their human-centric nature, host a surprising variety of insects, such as cockroaches, houseflies, and even bees, that have adapted to city life, demonstrating evolutionary flexibility and ecological plasticity.

Understanding the life cycles of different insects is essential to appreciating their biological and ecological roles. Insect life cycles vary significantly across species but generally include stages such as egg, larva, pupa, and adult. For instance, butterflies undergo complete metamorphosis, beginning as eggs that hatch into caterpillars (larvae) before transforming into pupae and finally emerging as adults. This dramatic transition not only enables resource partitioning but also reduces competition between juvenile and adult stages. Similarly, many beetles and flies exhibit complete metamorphosis, each stage adapted to different ecological niches.

Conversely, insects like grasshoppers and cockroaches go through incomplete metamorphosis, skipping the pupal stage and gradually developing into adults through a series of nymphal stages. This process provides a constant presence in their habitat, allowing for continuous interaction with their environment. Understanding these life cycles is crucial for pest management strategies and conservation efforts, as it helps identify vulnerable stages where intervention can be most effective.

Preserving diverse habitats is paramount to maintaining healthy insect populations. Habitat loss due to urbanisation, agriculture, and climate change poses a significant threat to insect diversity worldwide. Protecting and restoring diverse habitats ensures that insects continue to perform essential ecological functions such as pollination, decomposition, and serving as food for other wildlife. For example, conserving wetlands supports dragonfly and damselfly populations, which in turn control mosquito numbers and benefit amphibian and bird species that rely on them for food. Similarly, maintaining forested areas preserves the intricate web of interactions involving decomposers like beetles and detritivores such as ants, which recycle nutrients and sustain soil health.

Effective conservation strategies must integrate habitat preservation with sustainable practices. Agricultural landscapes can be managed to support both crop production and insect health by incorporating pollinator-friendly plants, reducing pesticide use, and maintaining hedgerows and natural buffers. Urban planners can design green spaces that provide habitats for butterflies, bees, and other beneficial insects, enhancing biodiversity within cityscapes. Climate change mitigation efforts should consider the impacts on insect populations, ensuring that warming temperatures and altered precipitation patterns do not disrupt the delicate balance of ecosystems reliant on insect diversity.

Ecological Roles: The Importance of Insects in Ecosystems

Insects play an irreplaceable role in maintaining the ecological balance of our planet. From pollination to decomposition, they are integral to various processes that sustain life as we know it. Understanding these roles is essential for appreciating the true value of insects and recognising the need for their conservation.

The Role of Insects as Pollinators

Insects play a very important role in the world, especially when it comes to pollination. Pollination is the process by which pollen is transferred from one flower to another. This process helps flowers and plants reproduce. Many kinds of insects join in this task, including bees, butterflies, beetles, and other small creatures. Each of these insects contributes in its own way, and without them, many plants would not be able to reproduce at all.

When bees land on a flower, they collect pollen on their bodies and move it to another flower when they go looking for more food. This simple act of moving from flower to flower is crucial for many plants, as it allows them to produce seeds and fruits. For example, when bees pollinate apple trees, they help to produce the apples that we all enjoy. Butterflies and beetles also play a role in this process. Like bees, they visit flowers to gather nectar and pollen, and in doing so, they help plants grow and thrive.

Pollination is essential not just for wild plants but also for crops that we rely on for food. In fact, an estimated 75% of the world's flowering plants and about 35% of food crops depend on animals, particularly insects, to reproduce. This means that many of the fruits and vegetables we eat would not be possible without the help of these tiny but important creatures. Think about the strawberries, almonds, and pumpkins you enjoy; all of these crops require pollination. Without pollinators, our diet would look very different, and many of these foods would be scarce or completely unavailable.

The significance of insect pollination goes beyond just the availability of food. It also has huge economic implications. Agriculture relies heavily on the work of pollinators. The production of fruits, vegetables, and nuts contributes billions of dollars to the economy worldwide. For farmers, having pollinators is essential to ensuring that their crops produce enough fruit. If crop yields drop because pollinators are missing, farmers may find it hard to make a living. Thus, there exists a strong link between the health of insect populations and the economy on a broader scale.

Insect pollinators also support biodiversity in ecosystems. Biodiversity refers to the variety of living organisms in a place. Healthy ecosystems with diverse plants are more resilient and can adapt better to changes in the environment, like climate change or disease. When pollinators help in the reproduction of flowering plants, they contribute to the richness of an ecosystem. This richness leads to a variety of habitats and food sources for many animals. If insect populations were to decline, many flowering plants would also struggle to survive, leading to a ripple effect that could harm entire ecosystems.

For instance, consider the community of plants and animals that exist in a forest. Each plant plays a role in providing food and shelter for various animals. Bees, butterflies, and beetles help to keep this plant community robust by ensuring that plants reproduce and grow. If one species of plant were to decline because it lost its pollinators, it could cause other species that rely on it for survival to also decrease. This interdependence showcases just how connected all the living things in an ecosystem are.

Understanding the role of insect pollinators highlights their importance in agriculture and our daily lives. Pollinators provide not just food but a variety of options that enrich our diets. Without them, our meals would lack variety, and many filling and nutritious foods might be entirely missing from grocery stores. Fruits and vegetables are essential in promoting good health, and their availability often depends on the health of pollinator populations.

To protect and promote pollination, communities and individuals can take simple steps. Planting native flowers in gardens can help attract bees and butterflies. Creating spaces for pollinators to thrive, like meadows or wildflower gardens, can enhance local environments. Reducing pesticide use is key, as many chemicals can harm these beneficial insects. Awareness is also crucial. The more people know about how vital pollinators are, the more likely they are to help preserve their habitats.

It is clear that insects and their pollination activities hold great importance in maintaining our ecosystems and supporting agriculture. The economic value derived from these pollinators represents an important part of farming and food production. Humans and these tiny creatures are connected in a variety of ways, showing just how essential they are for healthy environments and communities. By supporting and protecting insect pollinators, we can help ensure a sustainable and diverse food supply for the future.

In addition to their role as pollinators, insects such as beetles, flies, and ants are crucial decomposers.

They break down dead plant and animal matter, recycling it into soil nutrients. This decomposition process is vital for soil health and fertility, ensuring that nutrients are available for new plant growth. Without insect decomposers, dead material would accumulate, leading to nutrient lock-up and rendering them unavailable to the ecosystem. For instance, dung beetles play a pivotal role by consuming and breaking down faeces, thereby cleaning the environment and returning essential nutrients to the soil. This nutrient cycling supports plant growth and overall environmental health, making decomposers indispensable components of ecosystems.

The contribution of insects to nutrient cycling extends beyond decomposition. Many insects consume organic materials, dissolving them into simpler compounds that plants and other organisms can easily absorb. Termites, for example, digest cellulose in wood, turning it into simpler substances that enrich the soil. This continuous breakdown and redistribution of nutrients helps maintain soil structure and fertility, supporting diverse plant communities and the animals that depend on them. By fostering the healthy soil conditions required for robust vegetation, insect-facilitated nutrient cycling ensures the sustainability of ecosystems.

The interconnectedness of insect life with other environmental components cannot be overstated. Insects occupy fundamental positions in the food web, serving as prey for numerous animals, including birds, reptiles, amphibians, and mammals. Their abundance and diversity make them a critical food resource for many predators. The decline of insect populations could initiate a cascade of negative effects through the food chain, impacting predators and the ecosystems they inhabit. For example, a decrease in insect numbers could lead to reduced bird populations, which, in turn, might affect seed dispersal and plant growth. The intricate relationships between insects and other species illustrate the delicate balance of nature and the far-reaching consequences of disruptions in insect populations.

Dr. Anthonysamy David

Human activities have increasingly threatened insect populations worldwide. Habitat loss due to deforestation, urbanisation, and agricultural expansion reduces the available living space for insects, while pollution, pesticide use, and climate change further exacerbate their decline. These challenges highlight the urgent need for conservation efforts to protect insect habitats and mitigate human impacts. Conserving insect diversity is paramount for maintaining the stability and functionality of ecosystems. Protecting natural habitats and adopting sustainable practices in agriculture and forestry can help preserve the myriad roles insects play.

Educational Content: Insights into Insect Biology and Behaviour

Insect biology and behaviour offer a fascinating study into the diverse adaptations, behaviours, and evolutionary history of one of the most successful groups of organisms on Earth. Insects have evolved an array of specialised features that enable them to thrive in virtually every habitat on our planet. This subpoint aims to shed light on these adaptations, delve into their intriguing behaviours, and explore their evolutionary journey through millions of years.

One of the most remarkable aspects of insect biology is their specialised adaptations. Insects exhibit a wide variety of mouthparts tailored to their specific diets. For instance, butterflies and moths possess a long, coiled proboscis for sipping nectar from flowers, while beetles have robust mandibles for chewing plant material or prey. These mouthparts are the result of evolutionary modifications that allow insects to exploit different food sources efficiently. Additionally, insects are the only invertebrates capable of flight, a feature that has significantly contributed to their evolutionary success. Their wings, which vary dramatically in structure and function, enable them to escape predators, search for food, and find mates. Some insects, like beetles, have hardened forewings called elytra that protect their delicate hindwings and body, while others, like dragonflies, possess two pairs of powerful, membranous wings that allow agile flight.

Another notable adaptation is the protective exoskeleton. Insects possess an external skeleton made of chitin, which provides both support and protection. This exoskeleton is segmented into distinct parts: the head, thorax, and abdomen, each serving specific functions. The head houses sensory organs such as antennae and compound eyes; the thorax supports legs and wings; and the abdomen contains vital systems like digestion and reproduction. The exoskeleton also prevents water loss, allowing insects to inhabit dry environments successfully.

In addition to physical adaptations, insects display a wide range of fascinating behaviours. Mating rituals among insects are particularly diverse and often elaborate. For example, fireflies use bioluminescence to attract mates, with males and females flashing species-specific patterns in the dark. In contrast, some male insects engage in combat to win the attention of females, as seen in certain beetle species, where males wrestle using their enlarged mandibles. Social structures in insects, such as those found in bees, ants, and termites, also highlight complex behaviours. Honeybees live in highly organised colonies where each member has a specific role, from workers gathering nectar and pollen to the queen laying eggs. This social organisation ensures the colony's survival and efficiency.

Feeding habits among insects are equally varied. Predatory insects like praying mantises hunt other insects with precision, using their raptorial front legs to capture prey. Herbivorous insects, such as caterpillars, consume plant material and can sometimes be significant agricultural pests due to their voracious appetites. Detritivorous insects, like dung beetles, play a crucial role in breaking down and recycling organic material, thus contributing to nutrient cycling in ecosystems.

The evolutionary perspective of insects reveals a long and intricate history of adaptation and diversification. Fossil records indicate that insects first appeared around 480 million years ago, during the Ordovician period. Over millions of years, they have undergone significant evolutionary changes, leading to the immense diversity we see today. The development of flight about 400 million years ago was a major milestone in insect evolution, granting them access to new habitats and resources, which in turn propelled further diversification. The adaptability of insects to various environmental conditions has allowed them to colonise nearly every terrestrial ecosystem, from arid deserts to dense forests.

Understanding the evolutionary history of insects also involves examining their relationships with other organisms. Co-evolution is evident in the mutualistic relationships between insects and plants, such as pollination. Bees, butterflies, and other pollinators have evolved alongside flowering plants, resulting in intricate adaptations that benefit both groups. For example, many flowers have evolved bright colours and specific shapes to attract pollinators, while insects have developed specialised structures to access nectar and transport pollen.

Making Complex Scientific Concepts Easy to Understand

Presenting complex scientific concepts in a way that is easy to understand is very important. This approach helps to engage a wide range of people, whether they are students, teachers, or just curious readers. When scientific information is made accessible, it encourages more people to learn and explore different topics in science. The goal is to help everyone grasp the main ideas without feeling overwhelmed by difficult terms or ideas.

One effective method to simplify technical terms is to use relatable analogies. Analogies are comparisons that help to illustrate a point, making it easier for readers to connect with the content. For example, when explaining the specialised mouthparts of insects, one might compare them to different kitchen utensils. Just as a fork is designed for picking up food and a knife is used for cutting, insects have mouthparts that are tailored for their specific feeding needs. For instance, a butterfly has a long, straw-like proboscis that allows it to sip nectar from flowers, much like using a straw to drink juice. This kind of comparison helps readers visualise and understand how these adaptations serve a purpose in the insect's life.

Understanding Insect Mouthparts

To further clarify the concept of insect mouthparts, let's look at a few different types. For example, some beetles have jaws that are strong and designed for chewing, similar to how a pair of scissors works to cut paper. These beetles need to munch on leaves or wood, and their mouthparts are perfectly suited for that task. On the other hand, mosquitoes have a more specialised structure that allows them to pierce the skin of animals and humans to take a blood meal.

In each case, the unique shape and function of the mouthparts allow insects to feed effectively within their environment. Using examples from everyday kitchen items helps to break down technical language into something more familiar to readers, enabling them to grasp the important concepts about how adaptations work in nature.

Exploring Social Organisation Through Teamwork

Another complex topic is the social organisation of honeybees. Honeybees are known for their highly structured communities, which can be likened to a well-coordinated team working towards a common goal. Each bee has its own role within the hive, much like players on a sports team. The queen bee is similar to a team captain—she is responsible for laying eggs and maintaining the population of the hive. Worker bees, on the other hand, take on various tasks, such as foraging for food, building the hive, or caring for the young.

When people think about bee behaviour, they often wonder how such small creatures coordinate their activities so effectively. By comparing these behaviours to those of a sports team, one can illustrate how teamwork enables the hive to function smoothly. For example, when a worker bee finds a source of nectar, she performs a special dance to show others where it is located. This may remind us of how players might communicate during a game strategy session, working together to achieve a win.

The Importance of Team Roles

Moreover, just as every player has a position on a sports team, every bee has a specific job that contributes to the hive's overall success. For instance, nurse bees focus on feeding and nurturing the larvae, while guard bees protect the entrance from enemies. This division of labour ensures that the hive remains functional and safe. By using clear examples and straightforward comparisons, readers can better appreciate the complexity of bee social structures without getting bogged down in scientific jargon.

Understanding these social dynamics within a colony gives readers insights into how nature operates. It showcases the interdependence that exists in ecosystems, providing a deeper understanding of the role each species plays within the larger picture.

Making Science Relatable

When discussing complex scientific concepts, the ultimate aim is to engage and inform the audience. Relatable language and analogies serve as powerful tools in this endeavour. By relating intricate topics to everyday situations and objects, we can open doors to understanding and appreciation for science in our daily lives.

The key is to continue exploring ways to make science relatable. We can achieve this by thinking of common experiences while teaching or explaining science. Whether it's through sports team strategies or the tools we use in the kitchen, these everyday items and experiences can act as bridges that connect abstract scientific ideas with real-life contexts.

As a result, readers are more likely to retain information and find joy in learning about nature and science. When individuals feel that they can understand complex topics, it not only enhances their knowledge but also nurtures a curiosity that might lead them to explore even further into scientific realms.

Using clear definitions, relatable examples, and approachable language fosters an environment where learning feels less daunting. This way, readers are empowered to delve deeper into subjects that once seemed inaccessible. By demystifying science, we help shape a more informed and inspired audience that values and actively engages with the wonders of the world around them.

Photographic tours of insects can also enhance understanding by visually illustrating these biological and behavioural traits. High-quality images capturing the intricate details of insect anatomy, such as the texture of their exoskeletons or the structure of their compound eyes, can make the text more engaging and informative. Dynamic photos showcasing behaviours like mating displays or feeding interactions can further enrich the reader's experience, offering a glimpse into the vibrant lives of insects beyond static descriptions.

Global Perspective: A Comprehensive View of Insect Diversity

Insects comprise nearly 80% of the world's known species, reflecting their immense diversity and significance in various ecosystems. This section focusses on offering a global perspective on insect diversity while addressing pertinent conservation challenges affecting these vital organisms.

First, it is essential to appreciate the global nature of insect diversity. Insects inhabit nearly every corner of the Earth, from the dense tropical rainforests of the Amazon to the arid deserts of Africa and the frozen tundras of the Arctic. This vast distribution exemplifies their adaptability and evolutionary success. For instance, the unique fauna of Madagascar features over twelve thousand insect species found nowhere else on the planet, showcasing the island's isolated evolution. Similarly, the Australian continent boasts an array of indigenous insects, like the vibrant jewel beetles and diverse ant species.

Beyond merely cataloguing insects, understanding their roles within different cultural and ecological contexts enhances our appreciation of their ubiquity. Various societies perceive and utilise insects differently, often rooted in traditional practices and beliefs. In many African communities, termites are not only considered a food source but also play an integral role in soil aeration and nutrient cycling. In Japan, insect husbandry, particularly with beetles and crickets, has long been part of cultural activities and remains popular today (Donkersley et al., 2022). Such cultural perspectives underline the multifaceted relationships humans share with insects, extending beyond utilitarian purposes to encompass social and spiritual dimensions.

Ecologically, insects serve as fundamental components in myriad processes. Pollinators such as bees and butterflies perform critical functions in maintaining plant biodiversity and agricultural productivity. Without them, many crops and wildflowers would fail to reproduce. Herbivorous insects help control vegetation growth, while predatory insects maintain the balance of pest populations, preventing outbreaks that could devastate crops and natural flora. Decomposers, including various beetle and fly larvae, facilitate the breakdown of organic matter, recycling nutrients back into the ecosystem. These roles highlight the intrinsic value insects provide across multiple environmental services.

However, despite their significance, many insect species face severe conservation challenges threatening their survival. Habitat loss due to deforestation, urbanisation, and agricultural expansion remains a primary driver of insect decline. As natural habitats diminish, so do the resources and conditions necessary for insects to thrive. Fragmented landscapes result in isolated populations, diminishing genetic diversity and resilience against environmental changes.

Dr. Anthonysamy David

Another significant threat comes from climate change, which alters temperature and precipitation patterns, impacting insect physiology, development, and distribution (Kleber Del-Claro et al., 2024). For example, increased temperatures can disrupt the synchrony between pollinators and flowering plants, leading to reduced pollination success. Additionally, extreme weather events, such as droughts and floods, can decimate insect populations unable to adapt rapidly to such changes.

The pervasive use of pesticides poses another critical challenge, affecting both target pests and non-target beneficial insects. Modern agricultural practices heavily rely on chemicals that indiscriminately kill insects, reducing biodiversity and disrupting ecological balances. These chemicals accumulate in the environment, causing long-term detrimental effects on insect health and reproduction. Studies show that even sub-lethal doses of pesticides can impair cognitive functions in bees, undermining their ability to forage and return to their hives.

Addressing these conservation challenges requires a multifaceted approach that includes scientific research, public education, and policy interventions. Entomologists play a crucial role in advancing our understanding of insect biology and ecology, providing valuable insights that inform conservation strategies. Initiatives like citizen science programmes engage the public in monitoring insect populations, fostering awareness and stewardship at the community level (Donkersley et al., 2022).

Furthermore, implementing sustainable agricultural practices can mitigate the negative impacts of pesticide use. Integrated Pest Management (IPM) methods, which use biological control, habitat manipulation, and little to no chemical inputs, are good options that protect both plant and insect life. Promoting organic farming and reducing chemical dependencies align agricultural productivity with ecological preservation, ensuring long-term sustainability.

Increased efforts towards habitat restoration and protection are paramount. Establishing protected areas, rewilding degraded lands, and creating ecological corridors enhance habitat connectivity, allowing insect populations to disperse and maintain genetic diversity. Urban planning should incorporate green spaces and pollinator-friendly gardens, providing refuges for insects within cityscapes. Public pollinator gardens have become important conservation resources, demonstrating how small-scale initiatives contribute to broader ecological goals (Phillips et al., 2020).

At the policy level, developing coherent frameworks for insect conservation is essential. Governments worldwide need to extend protective measures beyond well-known pollinators like bees to include a vast array of less conspicuous but equally important insects. International cooperation and agreements can drive collective actions addressing transboundary issues such as climate change and pesticide regulation.

Final Thoughts

This chapter has thoroughly examined the diverse world of insects through vivid photography and insightful descriptions. By highlighting the intricate anatomical structures, unique colouration, and dynamic behaviours of various insect species, we have gained a deeper understanding of their evolutionary adaptations and ecological roles. These high-quality images not only showcase the beauty and complexity of insect life but also serve as valuable tools for research and education. They provide a visual gateway into the fascinating lives of these creatures, enhancing both scientific knowledge and general appreciation.

Additionally, the chapter has underscored the immense ecological importance of insects in various environments. From pollination and decomposition to their roles as prey and predators, insects are integral to maintaining the ecological balance. The photographs and accompanying text offer a comprehensive view of how insects interact with their habitats and contribute to ecosystem

Dr. Anthonysamy David

health. This dual focus on artistic presentation and scientific detail invites readers to appreciate insects not merely as visual subjects but as critical players in our natural world, thereby encouraging conservation efforts and informed environmental stewardship.

Reference List

11.11: Insects . (2016, October 5). Biology LibreTexts. https://bio.libretexts.org/Bookshelves/Introductory_and_General_Biology/Introductory_Biology_(CK-12)/11%3A_Invertebrates/11.11%3A_Insects

Bug Zoo. (2024, March 11). *The Critical Role of Insects in Ecosystems* . Bug Zoo Store; Bug Zoo Store. https://bugzoo.com/blogs/news/ecological-importance-of-insects

Chown, S. L., & Terblanche, J. S. (2006). *Physiological Diversity in Insects: Ecological and Evolutionary Contexts* . Advances in Insect Physiology. https://doi.org/10.1016/s0065-2806(06)33002-0

Donkersley, P., Ashton, L., Lamarre, G. P. A., & Segar, S. (2022, October). *Global insect decline is the result of wilful political failure: A battle plan for entomology* . Ecology and evolution. https://doi.org/10.1002/ece3.9417

Dr. Anthonysamy David

Insect Anatomy: An Overview | ScienceDirect Topics . (n.d.). Www.sciencedirect.com. https://www.sciencedirect.com/topics/agricultural-and-biological-sciences/insect-anatomy

Kleber Del-Claro, Miguel, Calixto, E. S., Centeno, E., Pereira, I., Anjos, D., Helena Maura Torezan-Silingardi, & Renan Fernandes Moura. (2024, March 5). *Evidence of climate change effects on insect diversity* . Oxford University Press EBooks; Oxford University Press. https://doi.org/10.1093/oso/9780192864161.003.0010

Samways, M. J., Barton, P. S., Birkhofer, K., Chichorro, F., Deacon, C., Fartmann, T., Fukushima, C. S., Gaigher, R., Habel, J. C., Hallmann, C. A., Hill, M. J., Hochkirch, A., Kaila, L., Kwak, M. L., Maes, D., Mammola, S., Noriega, J. A., Orfinger, A. B., Pedraza, F., & Pryke, J. S. (2020, February). *Solutions for humanity on how to conserve insects* . Biological Conservation. https://doi.org/10.1016/j.biocon.2020.108427

Song, B.-M., & Lee, C.-H. (2018, February 23). *Towards a Mechanistic Understanding of Colour Vision in Insects* . Frontiers in Neural Circuits. https://doi.org/10.3389/fncir.2018.00016

Verma, R. C., Waseem, M. A., Sharma, N., Bharathi, K., & Singh, B. V. (2023). *The role of insects in ecosystems: An in-depth review of entomological research* . International Journal of Environment and Climate Change , 13(10), 4340–4348. https://doi.org/10.9734/ijecc/2023/v13i103110

Wigglesworth, V. B. (2019). *Insects: Definition, Facts, and Classification* . Encyclopædia Britannica. https://www.britannica.com/animal/insect

www.ingramcontent.com/pod-product-compliance
Lightning Source LLC
Chambersburg PA
CBHW042045150726
48005CB00034B/1820